MAKE IT IN CLAY

Primal

Oozing mire, vital, electric.
Primordial.
Permeating all existence.
    repository of fossil memories.
Finger of creation, cosmic fire
    breathing life into Adam.
Expressions, impressions, marks
    Neolithic to Modern.
Yielding to plastic manipulations
    Vessels, idols, sun dried bricks.
Çatalhöyük first brick city,
    bull shrines,
    cities of the plain.
Babylonian ziggurats,
    cuneiform tablets
    transmitting tales
    of creation and profit.

Clay.

Mother.

—LOURDAN KIMBRELL

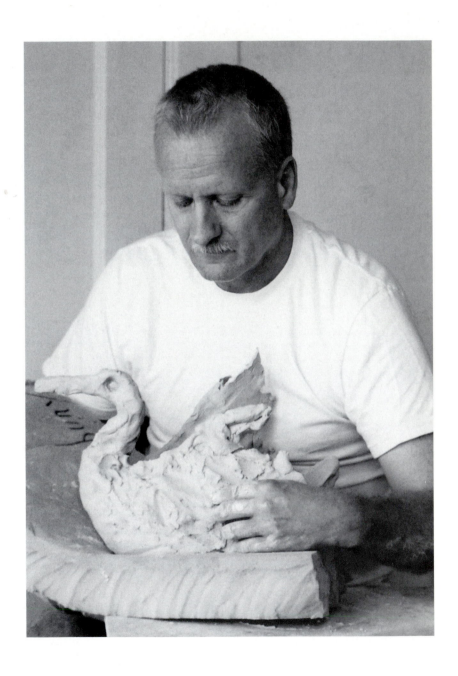

MAKE IT IN CLAY
A Beginner's Guide to Ceramics

SECOND EDITION

Charlotte F. Speight

John Toki
CALIFORNIA COLLEGE OF ARTS AND CRAFTS

MAYFIELD PUBLISHING COMPANY

MOUNTAIN VIEW, CALIFORNIA
LONDON • TORONTO

Library of Congress Cataloging-in-Publication Data

Speight, Charlotte F.
    Make it in clay : a beginner's guide to ceramics / Charlotte F. Speight, John Toki.—2nd ed.
      p. cm.
    Includes bibliographical references and index.
    ISBN 0-7674-1701-1
    1. Pottery craft. I. Toki, John. II. Title.
TT920.S687   2000
738—dc21   00-058672

Manufactured in the United States of America
10 9 8 7 6 5 4 3 2

Mayfield Publishing Company
1280 Villa Street
Mountain View, California 94041

Sponsoring editor, Janet M. Beatty; manuscript editor, Margaret Moore; design manager and cover designer, Susan Breitbard; art editor, Rennie Evans; illustrators, Emma Ghiselli, Judith Ogus, and John and Judy Walker; manufacturing manager, Randy Hurst. The text was set in 10/12 Melior by Thompson Type and printed on 70# Citation Gloss by Banta Book Group.

Cover photo by Anja Ulfeldt. Shown clockwise are Gavin Gilmore Kermode, Miel-Margarita Paredes, Dorothe Ursula Moller-Racke, and Arthur Gonzalez.

Preface

Make It in Clay introduces the beginner to the craft and art of ceramics. Designed for use in both beginning ceramics classrooms and studios, the text demonstrates the most basic techniques of the ceramic craft in step-by-step sequence. It also leads the reader to an appreciation of the *art* of working in clay. By offering photographs of experienced ceramists and students at work, along with a broad spectrum of professional contemporary ceramics, *Make It in Clay* inspires while it instructs.

The book moves in a progression from the simplest pinched pot to the finest thrown bowl, from an historic hand-sized figurine to a full-figure sculpture. More than 300 black and white photos and diagrams with detailed captions explain the intricacies of working with clay, and "Tips" include concise, positive advice for critical steps in the procedures. Chapter by chapter, the reader's knowledge and skill develop along with a greater and more discerning appreciation of the potential of ceramics.

Each chapter begins with illustrations of historical examples made using the processes demonstrated in that chapter. Readers will see how the world's most common earth material has been used to fulfill spiritual as well as utilitarian needs in the lives of people in all periods and cultures; they'll also see how our own ethnic roots may be reflected in the work of ancient craftspeople.

Thirty carefully chosen color plates illustrate the work of contemporary professionals who use the techniques taught in the book. By carrying the art and craft of ceramics to a high aesthetic and expressive level, these artists offer a glimpse of what readers may hope to achieve by continuing to work in clay. (This book enables students of ceramics to easily move on to *Hands in Clay,* where they will find the more advanced technical information necessary for proficiency in the field.)

v

FEATURES

Based on our own experiences as well as those of numerous ceramic artists and instructors we've spoken with, we've included these features that will be helpful to beginners:

- Because students often learn better by seeing an example of a process rather than reading a description of it, we've made the more than 300 illustrations as large as practicable, and we've limited the text to the most essential explanations.
- The spiral binding allows the book to lie flat for reference and will make it easier for a beginner ceramist to use the book in the studio.
- Space at the ends of chapters and at the end of the book encourages students to jot down notes, designs, sketches, or formulas.
- Basic tools, including professional, kitchen, and homemade ones, are shown in each chapter.
- Work illustrated is generally table-top in scale, easy to manage in weight and size.
- Helpful hints, called "Tips," are placed close to the pertinent illustrations and are indicated by this symbol: ⬤
- Safety symbols prominently placed in the margin alert users to appropriate precautions and specify the protective equipment for each process.
- Color plates are keyed to text or captions explaining forming, decorating, or firing processes.
- For inspiration, abundant illustrations of contemporary ceramic works and historical examples link the past to the present, showing cultural and ethnic diversity.
- A wide range of decorative methods offers an extensive palette for personal expression.
- An easy recipe introduces glaze chemicals and glaze testing.
- Kilns and kiln loading are demonstrated along with modern monitoring options.
- Raku firing dramatically demonstrates what happens when glazed ware is subjected to heat, fire, and a reduction atmosphere.
- Bold type for key terms and glossary references alerts readers to terms that may need explanation, highlighting essential information for review.
- Classroom-tested exercises at the ends of chapters suggest creative self-exploration through clay.
- A Further Reading list refers to specialized or advanced books for continuing exploration of ceramics.

NEW TO THIS EDITION

Here is an overview of what we've changed:

- **New profiles of artists:** A sculptor just starting out and two experienced potters talk about their professional lives: how they started and trained, what their influences were, and how they feel about their work.
- **Revamped chapter order and content:** Chapter 1 introduces the reader to the contemporary ceramic studio and its equipment. Chapter 2, "About Clay," describes the raw material from digging to recycling. Chapter 3, "Handbuilding," includes new pinching and coiling photos, and Chapter 4, "Slabs and Tiles," offers more detailed information on making tiles. Chapter 5, "Sculpture," illustrates new installations and mixed media works and features a chart of easily made armatures. Chapter 6, "Molds," contains detailed information on making and using molds, including multi-part molds. Chapter 7, "The Wheel," has been expanded with a new series on throwing a vase and now includes a chart showing wheel forms that can be made from basic cylinders. Chapter 8, "Surfaces," provides easy glaze recipes for the beginner and offers new dipping photos. Chapter 9, "Firing," has been expanded to discuss wood and salt firing.
- **New drawings:** Included are new drawings that clarify hand positions when working on the wheel; charts of studio equipment, firing equipment, technical drawings of kiln controls, a drying tent, and states of clay expand the beginner's familiarity with the studio and the material.
- **New recipes:** Beginners will find a number of new recipes for mixing and testing clay and for terra sigillata.

NOTE TO THE READER

Health and safety in the ceramics studio figure prominently in this book, and safety symbols placed in the margin, as shown here, alert readers to the need for precaution; the different symbols let readers know what protective equipment to wear for each process. The most up-to-date research in the field of ceramics forms the foundation of this book, and every effort has been made to provide appropriate warning where potentially hazardous substances or procedures are involved. Anyone following these procedures should use his or her best judgment and common sense. The authors and publisher shall not be liable in any event for incidental or consequential damages in connection with, or arising out of, the furnishing, performance, or use of the theories, procedures, and techniques herein.

ACKNOWLEDGMENTS

Our book was created with the help of the many ceramic artists who appear in its pages. From its inception, ceramists, students, and teachers have been generous with their time and their ideas. The book grew organically with their participation. To all of you whose works, photos, or ideas enrich the book, our sincerest thanks.

We'd especially like to thank the hundreds of instructors who responded to our questionnaire asking what specifics should be included in a basic book; we're also extremely grateful to the reviewers who provided invaluable suggestions on the manuscript as it developed: Bruce Amstutz, Shoreline Community College; Lisa Conway, University of Alaska, Anchorage; Cameron Covert, West Georgia College; Mark Derby, Newcomb College of Tulane University; William Disbro, Jamestown Community College; Kevin A. Hluch, Montgomery College, Rockville; Don D. Jennings, Orange Coast College; Robert Kibler, Glendale College; and James L. Tanner, Mankato State University. Thanks also to the reviewers of the second edition: Aurore Chabot, University of Arizona; David Foster, Lake Tahoe Community College; Barbara L. Frey, Texas A & M University, Commerce; Mike Hillman, Citrus College; John McCuistion, University of Puget Sound; Joe Molinaro, Eastern Kentucky University; and Marianne Weinberg-Benson, Kennesaw State University.

Special thanks to Steve Branfman of the Potter's Shop, Needham, Massachusetts, for sharing his expertise in the raku process and to all the sculptors and potters whose participation enriched the book. Their creativity will expand the reader's approach to clay.

We have a special relationship with our associates at Mayfield. It was senior editor Jan Beatty's idea to publish a concise ceramics text for beginners, and she convinced us of the need for such a book. Richard Greenberg, president, supported the idea and us as the authors for the project. Copyeditor Margaret Moore sharpened the writing and helped us make technicalities as clear as possible. The Mayfield production and art staff, especially Susan Breitbard, design manager and cover designer, and Anna George, designer, all contributed their skills to make the book visually inviting and attractive. Many thanks to all.

Contents

CHAPTER 1

The Ceramics Studio

The art and craft of forming, decorating, and firing **plastic** (malleable) **clay** into **pottery** or sculpture has had a lengthy history. Known as **ceramics,** it was one of the earliest—perhaps *the* earliest—technologies developed by humanity. The evolution of ceramics covers thousands of years and encompasses many cultures that were often separated by mountains, seas, and deserts. Around the world, at different times, numerous peoples discovered, or learned from trading with each other, that ceramics could ease or enrich their lives; the fired clay vessels that potters shaped could store or cook food efficiently, while sculpture expressed their feelings and recorded their daily lives and community beliefs.

EARLY POTTERY METHODS

Throughout history, people have formed clay by a variety of **handbuilding** methods (Chapter 3), in simple workshops or even sitting outside on the ground (1-1). Potters with no other tools but their hands or perhaps a piece of dried gourd or a smooth stone, **pinched** and **coiled** the clay and smoothed it into graceful pots that they decorated, perhaps with the imprint of their thumbs or braided cords or with mineral coloring materials (1-2). They fired these pots in open fires or in pits, and it was not until many centuries later that the true **potter's wheel** and the enclosed **kiln** were developed. Potters and sculptors still continue to shape clay with some of the same handbuilding methods in use thousands of years ago. To many of these **ceramists,** the sense of continuity with history is an important aspect of their interest in working in clay.

To most people, the word *ceramics* means household pottery or china (Color Plates 2, 10), but throughout history, ceramics has also contributed to human comfort or technology in the form of useful items such as water pipes or fired bricks for architectural uses, and floor and wall tiles for decoration (Color Plate 3). In the contemporary world, ceramics or ceramiclike materials are used for applications such as superconductors, silicon chips for computers, and tiles as insulation for spacecraft. Thus,

1-1 Around 1900 a Hopi potter sits on the ground, forming a pot on her lap, using the coiling method. Her damp clay beside her, she rests the pot on a basketry-mold, which will form a slightly rounded bottom on the pot. *Courtesy Museum of the American Indian, Heye Foundation, N.Y.*

the development of ceramics has contributed to technology around the world. Clay is also used in medicines, in cosmetics, and in the paper for this book. Because the earth has such abundant supplies of clay, ceramics will probably continue to have a place in our lives, even with the many humanmade materials now available.

Modern ceramists still use the same basic earth material, and many of the same forming methods as did early potters, but a modern studio that is equipped to produce a wide variety of **ceramic ware** also contains equipment that would be unfamiliar to a potter from, say, ancient Greece.

1-2 Water jars made in the American Southwest were built up with coils formed in a *puki,* a base-mold. Before firing, the clay was polished with a smooth stone. This jar was decorated in two shades of orange. Ht. 9¾ in. (25 cm). Teophilia Torivio?, Acoma, c. 1900? *Cat.# 12042/12: Ceramic jar, ca. 1900? Teophilia Torivio?, potter, Acoma. Arthur Taylor photo. Museum of Indian Arts and Culture/Laboratory of Anthropology, Santa Fe.*

THE CONTEMPORARY STUDIO

If this is your first visit to a modern ceramics studio, much of the equipment you see will be unfamiliar to you (1-3, 1-4). You may wonder if all of this equipment is necessary. Certainly, you could work sitting on the ground holding a lump of clay in your hands, pinching and coiling it into a small pot, but modern equipment makes the process of creating useful ceramic objects and sculpture easier and faster.

In order to take full advantage of the technological advances in ceramics that have been developed over centuries of experimentation, it is wise to become familiar with all that modern technology can offer you; then you can choose to work without it if you wish. We recommend, therefore, that you first spend some time in a well-equipped studio, learning the fundamentals from an experienced teacher. Your teacher can ease your way into the mysteries of ceramics, handing on much useful information from his or her own experience, as early potters taught their apprentices or as

1-3 Working in a ceramics studio at the California College of Arts and Crafts, Michael Prendergast throws a cylinder on the wheel. On the left, Chukes gives finishing touches to a portrait bust, while Rochelle Pendleton works on a tall coiled pot. The work of Sarah Kotzamani, Pam Dernham, and Karen Salinger can be seen on the shelves and windowsill. *Photo taken courtesy Ceramics Department, California College of Arts and Crafts.*

3

1-4 The well-equipped ceramics studio contains electric pottery wheels, a **slab roller,** wedging tables, a glazing area, gas and electric kilns, displays of artwork, a library, and a television for showing videos. Walnut Creek Civic Arts 7000-square-foot (653-square-meter) ceramics studio, managed by Peter Coussoulis. *Courtesy the City of Walnut Creek. Civic Arts Education Program, Walnut Creek Arts Center. Photo: David Hanney.*

1-5 Chart of equipment available in most school ceramics studios. ▶

children still learn from their parents in non-industrial cultures. It may take time to become familiar with the use of all the machines and appliances, and some of them require varying degrees of guidance from a teacher or technical assistant until you are familiar enough with them to use them on your own.

Ceramics Studio Equipment

The illustrations on the chart (1-5) will introduce you to many of the aids that may be available to help you to:

- prepare clay for use, following certain formulas so that the **clay body** you choose or mix will be appropriate for your type of work;

- **wedge** the clay to the exact consistency that is best for the forming method you choose;

- learn to work with ceramics materials in comfort, safety, and health;

- use various types of forming methods such as pinching, coiling, rolling out slabs, working on the potter's wheel, pouring **slip** into **molds;**

- discover what techniques are available to enhance the surface of your work through the use of texture, slips, **engobes, stains,** and **glazes;**

- fire your work, bringing the **ware** to **maturity,** according to the type of clay, decorative materials, and firing method you have chosen.

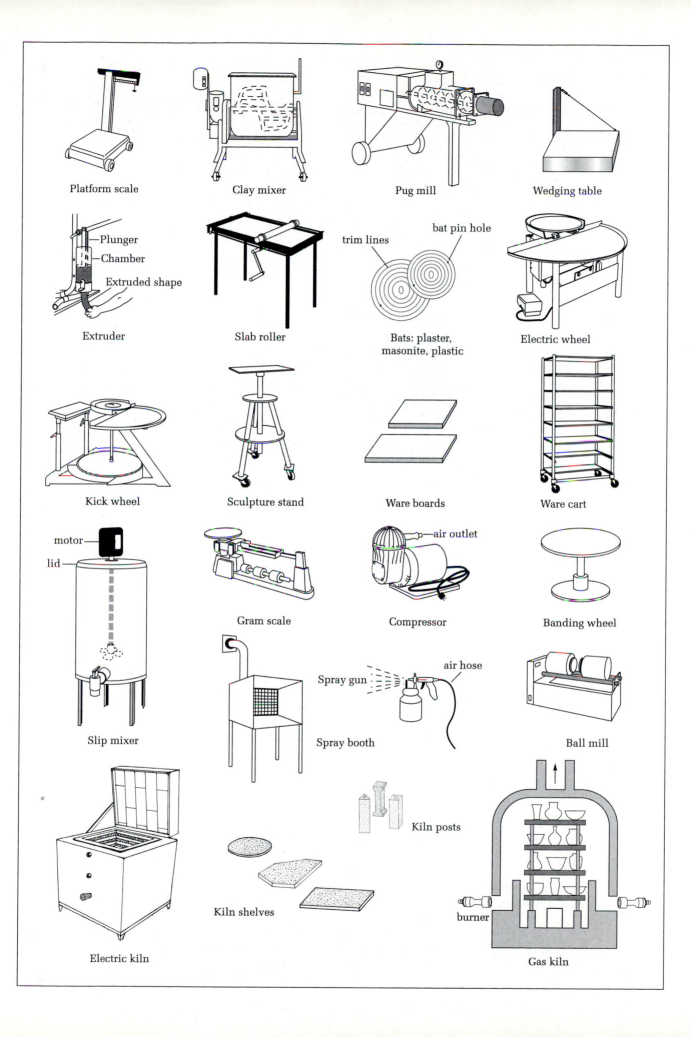

Platform scale

Clay mixer

Pug mill

Wedging table

Plunger
Chamber
Extruded shape

Extruder

Slab roller

trim lines
bat pin hole

Bats: plaster,
masonite, plastic

Electric wheel

Kick wheel

Sculpture stand

Ware boards

Ware cart

motor
lid

Slip mixer

Gram scale

air outlet

Compressor

Banding wheel

Spray booth

Spray gun
air hose

Ball mill

Electric kiln

Kiln shelves

Kiln posts

burner

Gas kiln

1-6 Emre Ucer, Turkey, unloads bisque ware from a computerized electric kiln. Computerized kilns can increase productivity and give potters better control over their bisque firings. *Courtesy the artist. Photo: Scott McCue.*

The following chapters will provide information about the chemistry and qualities of various types of clay (Chapter 2); about basic forming methods (Chapters 3 to 7); and about some of the techniques you can adopt to enhance the clay's surface (Chapter 8). Finally, Chapter 9 will take you through the process of preparing your work for the kiln, then firing it (1-6).

Throughout the book, we have generally illustrated pottery or sculpture of a size that is convenient for forming on a table, on a **banding wheel,** or on a potter's wheel. A few larger pieces are illustrated, however, that will suggest the wider possibilities of working in clay, to inspire you as you become more accomplished with the material.

KEY TERMS

plastic	clay body
clay	wedging
pottery	slip
ceramics	mold
handbuilding	engobe
pinching	stain
coiling	glaze
potter's wheel	ware
kiln	maturity
ceramists	banding wheel
ceramic ware	

NOTES/SKETCHES

CHAPTER **2**

About Clay

Clay, in its dry state, is a crumbly earth material that is soft and easily modeled (**plastic**) when wet, holds its shape when formed and dried, and then becomes a new, hard, dense material—ceramic—when subjected to heat and sufficient time in the kiln to reach maturity. It is these three characteristics of clay that you will make use of in your studio work. Once fired, ceramic can never be returned to its former state—clay.

Due to these three characteristics, in early cultures moist clay became an art material as well as an extremely useful material for producing food containers, bricks for building, and tiles for floors and roofs. The techniques for forming and firing clay were among humanity's first technological developments, and the technology of ceramics has influenced the growth of civilization.

HOW CLAY WAS FORMED

The rocks that cover much of the earth's surface are composed of minerals and compounds of elements (2-1). The two most essential minerals in clays and glazes are **silica** and **alumina.** It is these two minerals that make the ceramic process possible. Over millions of years, through the continuous action of weathering and geological forces, these **feldspathic** rocks were transformed both physically and chemically. The actions of rain, snow, frost, water, and wind all played their part in breaking the rock down into smaller and smaller grains. Then, as these particles traveled in streams and rivers, they picked up additional minerals, such as iron and copper. Other organic substances were also incorporated into the composition of the particles, all affecting the eventual

7

FROM ROCK TO POT

2-1   The journey of clay
from rock to pot.

The weathering of rain, snow, frost, and wind
breaks down mineral-bearing rocks into
pebbles, grains, and microscopic particles
which are then transported by streams,
glaciers, and rivers. Feldspar is the most
common clay-forming mineral, comprising
about 60 percent of the earth's crust.

Primary clay, a white heat-resistant material
known as kaolin, was deposited near the rocks
from which it derived. Due to geologic changes,
the mountains may have disappeared.

Glaciers and rivers move the smaller rock particles, which pick
up minerals and organic substances as they travel. Geologic
forces heave and tilt the earth, lakes dry out, and stream beds
change, leaving these **secondary clay** deposits exposed as fire
clay, stoneware, and earthenware.

Potters have been digging clay from
hills and stream banks for at least
12,000 years. They dried and cleaned
it, mixed it with water, and added
sand, mica, or ground-up fired pots
to open its pores.

With added water the clay becomes plastic again. When
it is formed into pots or sculptures, dried and exposed to
adequate heat, the chemical and physical composition of
the material changes—clay becomes ceramic.

characteristics of the final product—clay—and its malleability, texture, and color. Eventually, the clay particles settled into streambeds or along banks, which many millennia later reappear as clay deposits beside road cuts or along gullies where they have been transported by geological changes in the earth's crust. This explains why you may find a bank of clay far from any riverbed.

TYPES OF CLAY

Natural clays vary from place to place—a fact that helps archeologists analyze just where a particular piece of pottery was made. Clays are differentiated by the size of their particles, their color, and the minerals they contain.

There are two basic types of clay: the **primary clays,** which generally remain in beds near the rocks from which they were formed; and the **secondary clays,** which were deposited in beds far from the original rock. Natural clays of various composition are available around the world, and potters in nonindustrial societies continue to use these local clays. Even where commercially blended clay is available, some contemporary potters prefer to dig natural clays because they like to preserve a direct connection with the earth and with the continuum of ceramics history (2-2 to 2-6).

2-2 Digging natural clay. The abundance of earthenware clay and its ability to reach maturity at low temperatures in open or pit fires made it useful in early cultures, and it is still sought by ceramists today. Ellen Hall is a participant in the Indigenous Clay Workshop led by Professor Michael Peed at Montana State University, Bozeman. *All photos courtesy Michelle Tebay.*

2-3 Sifting the crumbled dry clay to remove pebbles and organic matter. In a less arid climate, indigenous clay would likely be dug in damp chunks, then dried, broken up, and crushed before it was sifted.

2-4 Peed and his students preferred to complete the process on site, dampening the clay to the plastic state. Some natural clays may need added material such as sand to open the pores and make them less likely to crack when subjected to heat.

2-5 Wedging indigenous clay. Peed says, *The clay contains mica and it worked fine without mixing in any additional material. This may be because we only screen it to "window" screen size so larger particles remain.*

2-6 To test the indigenous clay while still in the field, Peed pinched and coiled a pot in a *puki,* finding the clay usable without mixing in any additional material.

The deposits of natural clay are made up of varying types of clay that are differentiated by the size of their particles, their color, and the minerals they contain, which in turn affect the qualities of the clay. Some clays are naturally plastic and easy to form on the potter's wheel, whereas some are better adapted to handbuilding. For example, certain clays, especially red **terra-cotta,** are appropriate for flowerpots because after firing they are porous and hold moisture, whereas other fine-grained clays are light in color and contain **china clay.** These are suited for making table china.

In the past, when lack of transportation limited humans to the clay deposits they found close to their homes, the potters in an area would usually dig in the same place, and therefore they all would use the same kind of natural clay. Later, as transportation and trade developed and knowledge of clay ingredients was built up through experiment, potters were able to blend clay materials from other areas into their **clay bodies,** adapting them for specific purposes.

Now, after thousands of years of experimentation and chemical analysis, ceramists can choose from a wide variety of specially blended clays, among them porous red **earthenware,** which is fired at about 1900°F (1038°C); **stoneware,** which is impervious to water and acid when fired to maturity between 2100° and 2400°F (1148° and 1316°C); or **porcelain,** which is a white, smooth body typically fired at above 2380°F (1304°C). These clay types also differ in their plasticity and in their resistance to heat in the kiln. **Refractory** clay can resist high temperatures and long duration of firing without melting and deforming. It is used primarily in recipes for porcelain and stoneware, and also for building kilns and **kiln furniture.**

PREPARED CLAY BODIES

Commercially mixed clay bodies are blended and refined to perform in appropriate ways under certain forming techniques, to mature at various kiln temperatures, and to produce fired material with certain properties.

If you are using commercially mixed clay or a school clay body, it is blended and refined to perform in appropriate ways under certain forming processes, firing methods, and temperatures in the kiln. Various materials, such as **grog**—a ground-up fired ceramic material— may be added to the clay body to open up the clay's pores and to reduce shrinkage and warping during drying and firing. This additive is generally used when building large pieces of pottery or sculpture, which often contains up to 30 percent grog.

Although pre-mixed commercial clays are available to most of us, in nonindustrialized areas, where no factory-blended clays may exist, potters continue to use local clays they dig themselves. Even if you do not intend to use natural clay regularly, it is interesting to dig and test the natural clays you can usually find somewhere in the countryside around you.

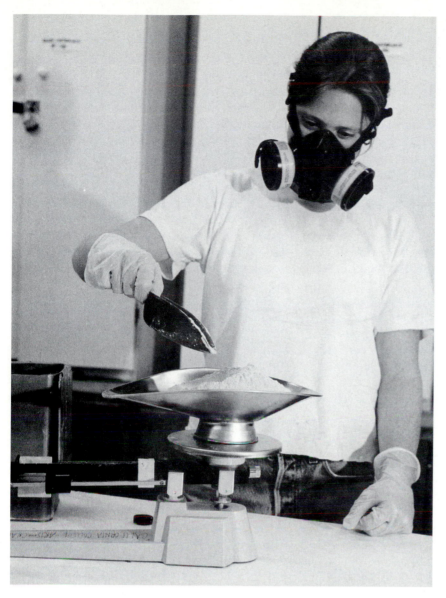

2-7 Wearing a respirator and gloves to protect herself against any dust from ceramics materials, Larissa Martin demonstrates the proper use of a respirator provided with the appropriate size of filter rated for dusts. The respirator should have a tight seal to your face.

HEALTH AND SAFETY

We know considerably more than early potters did about the safe uses of ceramics materials. Although school studios no longer use such toxic materials as lead, all ceramics materials should be used with care and the correct precautions taken (2-7). ***Before mixing or blending dry clay materials, be sure to read the health and safety instructions on page 12.***

Shield (shaded)

Goggles

Heat-resistant gloves

Waterproof gloves

Respirator

Personal health and safety equipment.

Studio Health and Safety Rules

- To avoid accidental ingestion of clay materials, never eat or smoke in the studio.

- Use the correct personal protection for each job. (Drawings in the margin will alert you to when and what type of protective equipment to wear.)

- Use respirators with a proper filter and tight seal between your face and the face piece.

- Replace respirator filters and clean respirators frequently, and store them in a clean plastic bag when not in use. Guidelines regarding kiln safety and protecting yourself during **raku** firing are given in Chapter 9.

Personal Protection

It is also important to protect yourself by using personal protective equipment. Whenever a process may require protection, one or more of the five drawings of protective equipment will appear near the text to tell you when you require extra care or protection. If you use the correct gear and follow the precautions carefully, you can work safely with clay and other ceramics materials. We have added some precautionary symbols next to some artists' photos to emphasize the need for being aware of health and safety matters.

Ventilation

Clay contains varying amounts of the mineral silica; thus, if trimmings from pottery or sculpture fall on the floor and are trampled to dust, or dry clay is sanded in the studio without proper removal of the dust, the microscopic silica particles in the clay dust will be diffused through the air. Breathed into the lungs over a long period of time, silica can cause various health problems. It is therefore essential that the clay studio have proper ventilation, and this is the reason studio cleanliness is vitally important.

School studios usually install powerful air-filtration systems that draw out the free-floating dust dispersed in the air from clay materials. Also, they may install fans over the particular areas where high concentrations of airborne particles or fumes are generated.

CLAY RECIPES TO MIX

Although in your work you may use only the clay that is mixed in your school or that comes from a clay company ready-mixed in a plastic bag, you will learn more about the constituents of clay and their proportions in a clay body if you mix a few clay recipes yourself. Following are recipes that you can mix in small quantities then form into tiles, mark with identifying numbers or letters, and test in a small test kiln if available.

Make It in Clay Cone 05, 5, and 10 Clay Bodies

	White Clay Cone 05 1915°F/1046°C	Buff Clay Cone 5 2185°F/1196°C	Buff Clay Cone 10 2381°F/1305°C
Components		Percent	
Kentucky ball clay (OM4)	50.0	50.0	28.0
Fire clay		30.0	52.0
Talc	50.0		
Grog (30–70 mesh) or Silica Sand (60–70 mesh)		20.0	20.0

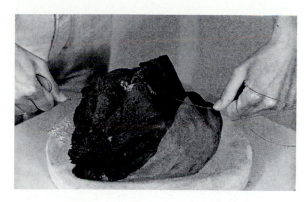

2-8 Try wedging two colors of clay together to see how wedged clay becomes homogenous.

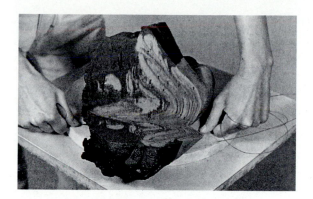

2-9 After a minute of wedging, cut the clay in half with a wire. Continue until the clay mass becomes marbled or reaches a total blend.

WEDGING

The clay you use when you begin to work may have been bought at the ceramic supply store or mixed to a school recipe, or you may have blended it from dry clay materials according to one or more of the recipes given above. In either of the first two situations, the clay will have been well blended and **de-aired** by mechanical means. For handbuilding, you could probably use the clay as it comes out of the bag, but it is good to get in the habit of **wedging** no matter what type of clay you are using or the type of work you will be doing.

By wedging you ensure that there are no air bubbles in the clay, that all the air is forced out, and that the clay is homogenous (2-8, 2-9). Eliminating air bubbles by wedging is especially important when **throwing** on the wheel because trapped air bubbles can cause a pot to become off center and the wall will then be uneven. Wedging also aligns the clay particles, creating a more homogenous mixture that helps prevent cracking or warping of slab-built work or thrown pottery during drying.

Sometimes a bag of clay has been sitting on a shelf too long and become stiff, or a tiny hole in the plastic may have allowed the air to enter and cause uneven stiffness. In either case, the clay needs to be reblended. Although clay that is kept for a long time in a cool place will become aged and more plastic, or malleable—especially good for throwing on the wheel—if you find the clay has dried and become too hard to work with easily, wrap it in damp cotton cloth or paper towels for two or three days—or at least overnight—until it is thor-

TIPS

Wedge porcelain and other white clay bodies on a clean surface to avoid color or particle contamination from differently colored or roughly textured clays.

Wedge clay on a solid, lower-than-normal surface so that

your upper body, arms, and hands will have more power and stability as you wedge.

If you are using bagged clay, pound it on a solid surface three or four times to help soften it before wedging.

oughly resaturated and can be wedged to homogeneity.

For handbuilding, you may use any method of wedging that works for you, but we recommend that you learn one of the traditional wedging techniques at the start, aligning the particles and making the clay into a compact ball, ready to use (2-10, 2-11, 2-12). Wedging on an absorbent surface such as a special plaster-topped wedging table or a surface covered with canvas will protect the clay from picking up any small chips of plaster that could cause problems after firing, when the chips can expand and come to the surface, pushing the clay or glaze off, leaving pockmarks on the surface.

A stretched wire attached to a wedging table allows you to cut the clay in half, slam the halves down again, and rewedge. If you do not have a wedging table, you can stretch a piece of canvas on any table and use a handheld wire to accomplish the cuts.

a

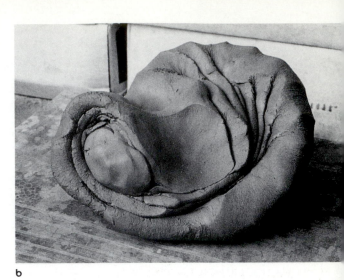

b

2-10 **a** Ron Judd, U.S.A., demonstrates wedging clay in the spiral method, on an absorbent wood surface. He uses a slight twist of the hands. This opens up all parts of the clay ball, allowing any air bubbles to escape.

b Spiral wedging also lines up the clay particles in the direction in which the pot will be thrown on the wheel.

 TIP

Wedge a few times to soften stiff bagged clay before you start to work with it.

2-11 Another method of wedging clay. Grasp a ball of clay, hold your arms firmly extended, push down and outward in a steady rhythmic motion, combining downward pressure with steady, applied force. Use the weight of your body and arms.

2-12 Turn the clay a quarter turn on each push, fingers curled inward. Push with a rolling motion, at least five times. Continue until the clay becomes a homogenous blend and resembles a ram's head.

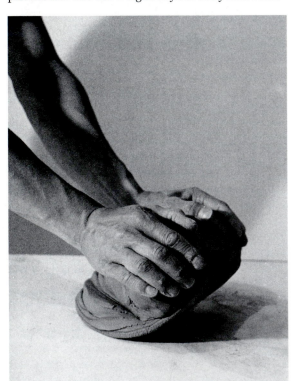

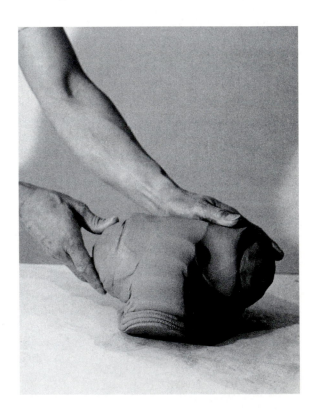

RECYCLING CLAY

Unfired clay trimmings and waste can be re-cycled using an effective recycling method used at Diablo Valley College in California. The system does not use any dangerous machinery, and is one that can easily be set up in the home studio.

The dry or damp clay scraps of one type of clay at a time can be saturated with water until they become a wet slop. This **slurry** is then placed on plaster or wooden bats, or on a concrete surface (2-13 to 2-17). The moisture in the clay is thus absorbed by the porous surface, and the clay is left until it is ready for wedging. Plaster absorbs the best, followed by wood and concrete.

2-13 Mark Messenger removes reclaimed wet clay from a bucket and begins to fill a plaster trough.

2-14 After the plaster trough is filled with clay it is left to dry for three to five days. The length of time in the trough is dictated by weather conditions and dryness of the mold. Once the clay has pulled away from the plaster wall by ¼" (6 mm), and the center is no longer wet, the entire block of clay is lifted from the trough and placed on a wedging table.

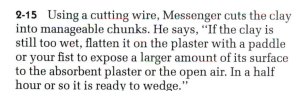

2-15 Using a cutting wire, Messenger cuts the clay into manageable chunks. He says, "If the clay is still too wet, flatten it on the plaster with a paddle or your fist to expose a larger amount of its surface to the absorbent plaster or the open air. In a half hour or so it is ready to wedge."

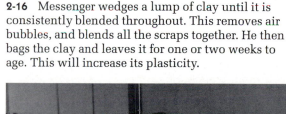

2-16 Messenger wedges a lump of clay until it is consistently blended throughout. This removes air bubbles, and blends all the scraps together. He then bags the clay and leaves it for one or two weeks to age. This will increase its plasticity.

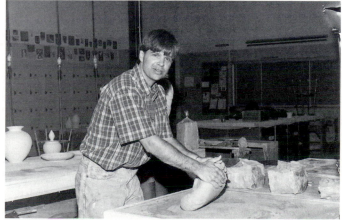

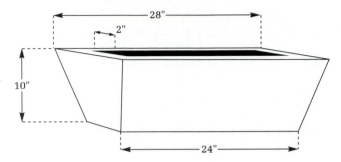

2-17 Plaster trough for drying clay slurry. The design works well because the entire chunk of clay dries out, including the center.

The next chapter will introduce you to some time-honored handbuilding methods that you can use to form clay into pottery or sculpture.

KEY TERMS

silica	porcelain
alumina	refractory
feldspar	kiln furniture
primary clay	grog
secondary clay	raku
terra-cotta	de-airing
china clay	wedging
clay body	throwing
earthenware	slurry
stoneware	

CREATIVE EXERCISE

Ask your state department of transportation or your college geology department for information on finding an accessible clay deposit. Dig some of the clay and shape it into a handsized sculpture or pot. To see how the clay changes color, texture, and size in the kiln, hollow out the sculpture if it is solid, dry your work, and fire it to cone 010.

NOTES/SKETCHES

CHAPTER **3**

Handbuilding

By now, you are well aware of the main characteristics of clay—plasticity, retention of shape as it dries, and transformation into ceramics if fired to maturity (Chapter 1). You have also learned about the qualities and constituents of clay, have mixed a clay body, and perhaps have tested it (Chapter 2). Thus, you have a theoretical background for working with the material. There is, of course, much more to learn about clay as you go further into ceramics, but now it is time to practice some forming techniques. This chapter and the following four chapters—Slabs and Tiles, Sculpture, Molds, and The Wheel—will introduce you to a number of forming methods. Whichever technique you choose, be sure to pick a clay that is adapted to the type of work you plan to produce; this will make your work a lot easier and the outcome more successful.

Before starting on a specific project, you may find it useful to play with the clay for a while as a child might and, in the process, find out just what it can or cannot do. Clay is an amazing material, very forgiving and responsive to being handled roughly or delicately.

Nevertheless, clay has its limits. By pinching or paddling it, rolling out slabs, then letting them slump, you can learn the possibilities as well as the limits of the material. Then you can follow your own ideas and discover that clay will carry the marks of your personality.

AESTHETIC CONSIDERATIONS

Don't restrict yourself too soon to one type of work or to one technique; try them all, and apply your aesthetic sensitivity to your work. Once you can control the clay, be aware of your pot's or sculpture's scale and profile, its overall mass, its separate forms, its volumes, as well as the negative spaces between them. The design of your work will be affected by subtle relationships between these elements as well as by surface texture and detail. How you make these relationships work together to create a pot that is satisfying to both visual and tactile senses will determine its success.

You will also be dealing with similar considerations in making sculpture, but in that

17

3-1 Formed thousands of years ago as a ritual object, this sculpture incorporates pinching and slab techniques, along with coils set up as columns. These simple techniques create a vivid picture of ancient ritual. The large, seated figures represent ancestors, or the deified dead, while smaller, standing figures place offerings on low tables. From the Phaestos region of Crete. *Photo taken with permission, Heraklion Museum, Crete.*

3-2 The Ibo, who lived west of the Niger River, placed sculptural pots on altars dedicated to Ifijiok, the Yam spirit. This pot shows images of the chiefs, their wives and children, and attendant musicians. Ht. 13¾ in. (35 cm). Ibo, Osisa, Nigeria. *Copyright British Museum.*

case you will probably be most interested in the expression of an emotion or idea. In addition, in making pottery or sculpture, you are creating actual forms in space. If you are working in three dimensions for the first time, this opens up other considerations that will be new to you and may take some getting used to.

HISTORY OF PINCHING

Holding a ball of clay in your hand is so compelling that it is difficult *not* to start pinching it. Pinching clay between fingers and thumb is a characteristic gesture that dates back to the earliest humans and appears to be a natural reaction to holding moist clay. Soft clay is seductive and so generally available in many areas of the world that it is quite likely early humans used it as a sculptural material even before they learned to fire it. In fact, deep in a cave in France, there is an image of bison made in damp clay that dates from the Ice Age.

The history of ceramics, however, began when humans realized that by firing a pot they had pinched from clay they had a container that could be used for food storage and for cooking certain foods in liquid to make them edible. They must also have become aware that by firing sculptured images they could preserve them for ritual use or possibly for children's play or instruction. For example, in

3-3 Animals were part of the daily life of early cultures and were often modeled as ritual vessels. Although this bull-shaped vessel realistically represents a domesticated animal, it has a pouring spout where the face would be, indicating it was probably used for libations. Amlash. First millennium B.C. *Copyright British Museum.*

3-4 Made on the island of Crete between 1700 and 1400 B.C., this large, fired clay storage vessel is called a *pithos*. Bands of applied decoration mark where new sections were added when the lower sections stiffened enough to support the weight of new clay. *Photo taken with permission, Heraklion Museum, Crete.*

the small clay shrine from Crete (3-1), notice that the heads of the deities or ancestor figures were formed by pinching the clay between thumb and forefinger. Ritual vessels like the Yam spirit pot (3-2), the pitcher shaped like a bull (3-3), and the Cretan storage jar, or *pithos* (3-4) were built in combinations of pinching, **coiling,** slabs, and **modeling.**

HANDS AS TOOLS

Your hands are the most useful and sensitive tools you will use in ceramics, so it is important to be aware of them and of your innate sense of touch. But as we have moved further and further away from a hands-on culture to an electronic world, our tactile sense may not be as responsive as that of early potters.

Try an experiment: With your eyes shut, touch and respond to as many textures and surfaces as you can find, reacting to the sensations and emotions they evoke. Explore, evaluate, and enjoy (or be revolted by) these surfaces. Increasing your tactile sensitivity in this way will enhance your work in clay, and you will find that gradually you will respond to ceramics as much through the touch of your fingers as through your eyes.

TOOLS

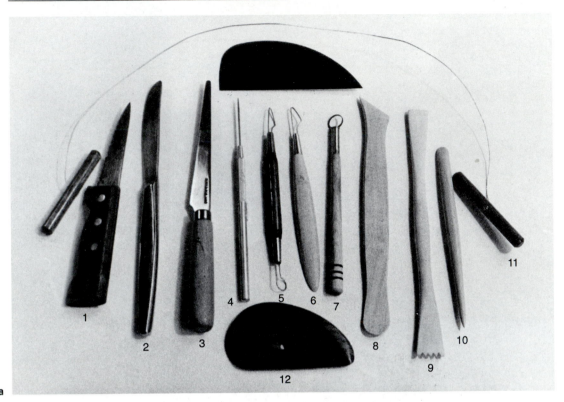

a

3-5 **a** Some basic handbuilding tools. In addition, you can make tools for your specific needs or adapt found objects to the type of work you are doing. (1) Paring knife. (2) Kitchen knife. (3) Fettling knife. (4) Needle tool. (5, 6, 7) Wire modeling/ trimming tools. (8, 9, 10) Wooden modeling tools. (11) Wire for cutting clay or removing work from bat. (12) Rib. **b** A collection of household objects that you may find useful when handbuilding.

TIP

Look in your kitchen, workshop, trash bin, or backyard, or on the beach for objects to use as tools. Your dentist may be willing to give you some old dental tools.

Collecting Tools

If you work only with your hands, the clay will preserve the mark of your fingers on the surface, recording their actions. At times, however, you will need a tool to reach into an area where your fingers cannot go, to slice into a form, or to smooth or texture the surface of the clay. Commercial tools (3-5a) are available for most specific needs, but you can also collect ordinary household objects to complete your tool set (3-5b).

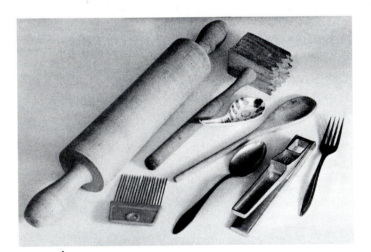

b

PINCHING

Pinching clay into a small, solid object such as a figure or a temple scene (3-1) presents no problem in firing since the clay is not too thick to fire solid, but if you try to form a sculpture significantly larger and thicker, you'll have to hollow it out so it will fire safely. (See Chapter 5.)

Instead of working solid, you can pinch the clay into an open form that you can then shape into a bowl (3-6 to 3-11), thinning out and smoothing the clay as you pinch the wall. Pinching in the hands of an expert can create lyrical, thin-walled pots (3-12, 3-13). If you prefer, you can finish the surface with tools. Such pinched forms can also be built as hollow sections of a large sculpture by melding them together, building the piece as large as you wish.

You can also close in the wall of a pinched form, making it into a hollow ball, then paddle or pound it into whatever shape you wish while the air pressure supports the wall (3-14 to 3-19). But don't fire a closed form without leaving a small hole in the wall to let the air and gases escape as it heats in the kiln.

3-6   Starting with a grapefruit-size ball of clay, Elizabeth Roberts begins a pinch pot by pushing her thumb into the center of the ball. *Photo: Kent Jolly.*

 TIP

Using a ball of clay about the size of an orange, maintain an even wall thickness as you pinch. A good gauge is the thickness of your thumb.

3-7   As she rotates the piece, she applies even pressure while pinching. This maintains consistent thickness of the walls.

3-8   As the pot increases in size, Roberts places it on a table and continues to pinch and turn the piece.

3-9 Once the piece reaches the desired size, she supports the interior wall with her left hand as she smooths the outside.

3-10 Roberts adds decorative elements and texture to the pinched pot, after letting it stiffen in the air for a short time.

3-11 After the basic pot was completed, Roberts altered the piece by pulling it into an oval shape. She added a handle to complete the piece.

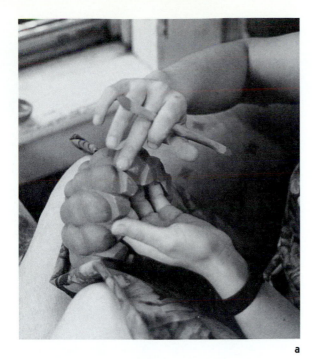

a

b

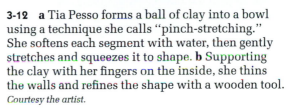
3-12 **a** Tia Pesso forms a ball of clay into a bowl using a technique she calls "pinch-stretching." She softens each segment with water, then gently stretches and squeezes it to shape. **b** Supporting the clay with her fingers on the inside, she thins the walls and refines the shape with a wooden tool. *Courtesy the artist.*

3-13 *Ocean Bowl 92B1T.* Pesso often spends up to fifty hours on one piece. She says, *I have a compulsion to thin the walls until they are consistent throughout, until the curving valleys, ridges, planes, and swells all flow without flaws to obstruct the movement of my fingers or offend my eyes.* Cone 10 stoneware, glazed inside. *Courtesy the artist. Photo: Tia Pesso.*

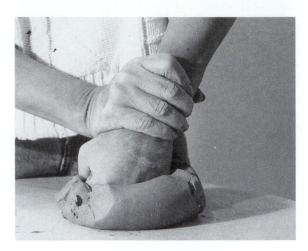

3-14   Using a method she learned from her Mexican assistant, Dina Angel-Wing opens her pinched pots with a punch of her fist. She then pinches the walls up with her fingers. Angel-Wing says, *It works well for forms that don't require too much handling or refining.*

 TIP

When pinching a closed form, shape it as near as you can to the form you want before pinching the walls together.

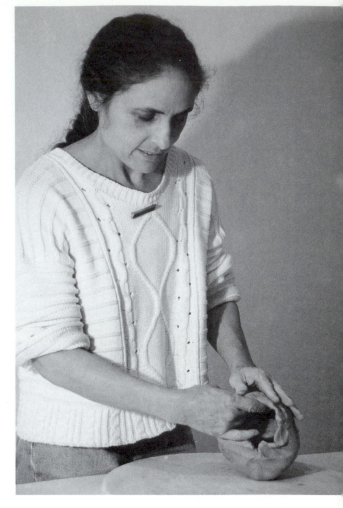

3-15   Angel-Wing next pinches and pulls the opened clay into a hollow shape from which she can make a vessel or a sculpture. *My assistant said this is how they make piñatas in Mexico. Before he taught me, I used newspapers to support the clay.*

3-16   Using moist clay that she can manipulate into shape in just a few moments, Angel-Wing pinches the walls. Keeping them a consistent thickness throughout, she folds and pushes, finally closing the walls completely, trapping air inside.

3-17   The trapped air supports the clay so that she can handle the piece quite roughly. She can pound the closed form on the table or drop it to change its shape without damaging it.

3-18 Angel-Wing paddles the closed form with quick strokes, both altering it and compressing the clay, which gives added strength to the walls.

 TIP

Wrap rough cloth, string, or a cord around a paddle. The texture will be imprinted in the damp clay as you paddle.

 TIP

Be sure to make a hole in a closed form before firing it.

3-19 When textured and fired, Angel-Wing's pinched and pounded pot becomes a rocklike flower vase, while other closed forms are decorative companion rocks. Just be sure you put a small hole in a closed form before firing it. This will allow steam and gases to escape. Speaking of the versatility of this way of working, Angel-Wing says, *I can cut into it, I can add on, I can turn something like this into a teapot if I want. Courtesy the artist. Photo: Frank Wing.*

a

3-20 **a** In a photo taken in the 1940s, Tewa potter Maria Martinez begins to coil a pot in a *puki*. San Ildefonso, New Mexico, c. 1940. **b** The fired earthenware *puki* helps to shape the bottom of the pot, making it easy to rotate. (1) The base is started in the *puki*. (2) Each new coil is carefully placed to shape the pot. (3) The walls are built consistent in thickness and (4) curved inward. The walls are then ribbed to final thickness. **a** *Photo by Wyatt Davis, courtesy Museum of New Mexico, neg. no. 68353.*

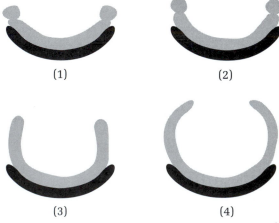

(1)   (2)

(3)   (4)

b

HISTORY OF COILING

Coiling, or a combination of pinching and coiling, is also an ancient technique, widely used around the world throughout ceramics history. Rough and primitive at first, coiled vessels were later refined into thin-walled, graceful vessels. There was a long tradition of hand-coiled pots around the world and on the American continents long before Europeans landed. Potters like Tewa potter Maria Martinez (3-20), in the North American Southwest, revitalized this ancient tradition of handcoiled pots. Martinez used a broken pot, or a specially formed and fired pot, called a *puki,* as a base **mold.** She would build up a pot with coils, pinching and melding the soft clay coils together as she shaped it. To develop the final shape of the pot and refine its surface, she used an old baking soda tin lid to scrape the pot smooth, then she **burnished** the surface with a smooth stone, both polishing it and tightening the pores. Other potters used mineral colors to decorate the surfaces of their pots.

MAKING THE COILS

It is easy to make coils. Choose whatever method works best for your project: Either squeeze thick clay in your hands until the coil is the desired thickness and length (3-21a) or roll the clay out in your hands or on a smooth, flat surface such as a table top (3-21b). Another way to make coils is by using an **extruder** (3-22), which pushes the clay through **dies** of various sizes and shapes to form solid or hollow extrusions (3-23). Coils can also be made as flattened strips of clay to be melded together into pots or sculpture by pinching. Whatever method you choose for making the coils, or whatever size the coils become, the process of building with them is basically the same. The important variable is the softness or stiffness of the clay; that can influence your method of attaching the coils to each other.

Coiling is adaptable to many types of work from small, delicate pieces that are smoothed with a rib so they show no indication of their coiled origins, to coils that are carefully joined but left unsmoothed in order to maintain the circling coils as a visual component of the piece. Both Juliet Thorne and Brian Gim roll

TIP

Apply even pressure with your hands on the coil as you roll it. Roll it thick and short or stretch it out thin and long.

3-21 a Squeezing clay into a long snake is one way to make thick coils, useful for large pots or sculpture. However, the uneven pressure of your fingers makes it difficult to keep the coils smooth. **b** Rolling coils on a smooth surface with the palm of your hand will give you greater control.

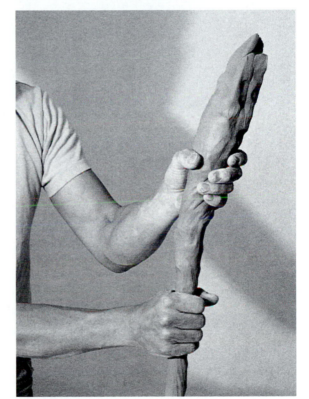

a

b

a

b

3-22 **a** Extruders are the fastest way to make coils of consistent thickness. **b** Rachel Ferreria uses thick, moist, extruded coils to form the walls of a sculpture, following an idea she drew in her sketchbook. As she builds, she melds the wet clay coils thoroughly together. Slip and scoring are not needed in this instance because the clay is very soft and sticks to itself when melded.

3-23 Coils and hollow tubes can be made quickly with an extruder, and extruded coils are the smoothest of all. You can make the coils thick or thin, depending on the die you insert in the extruder, and use them for numerous handbuilding methods.

thin, even coils by hand, carefully making them similar in size. This is particularly important in Thorne's work, since she does not meld or smooth the coils on the outside (3-25 to 3-31). In her figures, the spiraling coils are essential to the character of the piece (Color Plate 8). Gim, on the other hand, smoothes the surface with a rib (3-32 to 3-36), then alters the surface by paddling it with a piece of wood.

BUILDING WITH COILS

If the coils are really moist and pliable, you can simply press each new one onto a previous coil, melding them together with your thumb. This can be done successfully if the new clay is close in dampness to the coils to which it is being attached; then it is possible to smooth the walls with a **rib** (3-34), paddle it (3-36), alter its shape, and use it as a pot or even as the basis for a sculpture.

Juliet Thorne (3-25 to 3-31, Color Plate 8) uses two methods that differ from the standard coiling technique: She leaves the coils exposed on the outside, and she employs continuous coiling rather than using a one-coil-per-layer technique. This technique produces a strong sense of rhythm and movement as the viewer's eye is drawn up the figure by the spiraling action of the exposed coils. Although she uses this technique for figure sculpture, the same process could be used to build a pot by starting it on a slab base or in a rounded mold. Thorne prefers to work on two or more pieces simultaneously so that the newly coiled section of one will stiffen while she works on the other.

Scoring and Using Slip

If the clay is quite stiff, or if you want the coils to retain their form so that they create texture on the exterior, then the join will be more secure if you **score** the coiled surface with a sharp tool and paint it with **slip.** Do this by using a **needle tool,** a **scoring tool,** or even a kitchen fork, to scratch into the top surface of the preceding coil (3-24). Next, thoroughly spread slip mixed at about the consistency of

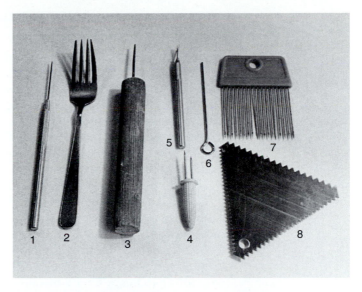

3-24 To score coils or slabs, use any scoring tool or kitchen object that works. **1** Needle tool. **2** Kitchen fork. **3** A favorite needle tool made by embedding a nail in a section of broom handle. **4** Corn holder. **5** Scoring tool. **6** Kitchen skewer. **7** Onion holder. **8** Serrated metal rib.

yogurt over the scoring. The coil is then ready for a new coil to be attached. If you find that the lower part of the piece is not firm enough to support the weight of clay you are adding, leave it to stiffen in the air for a while before adding more coils, always joining the new coils securely to the old.

As with pinching, you should try to build the coiled wall the same thickness throughout, or, if you prefer, scrape the wall to a consistent thickness after it has stiffened but is still workable. Ribbing the wall in this way with a rib not only will create a smooth surface (inside and/or out), but will ensure a tight bond between the coils. You can also paddle a coiled pot with a smooth or textured paddle or even a piece of wood (3-36), thereby altering the surface texture and helping to meld and compress the clay in the wall. Whatever method you use, just be sure that all the coils are well attached to each other so that they do not come apart or crack at the joins when drying. That is essential.

PROFILE Juliet Thorne

Juliet Thorne, who recently received an M.A. (By Project) in Art, Design, and Visual Culture at the London Guildhall University, started taking pottery classes on Saturdays while working in an office. She found her interest in sculpture deeper than her interest in pottery, and although she continued as a full-time ceramics student she did it to get a skill that would support her while she made sculpture. She soon realized that each was a full-time career, and each would take total concentration. Although she completed an undergraduate workshop ceramics course, by the time she finished, she says she was *just making torsos (exploring myself really).* (3-27 to 3-31, Color Plate 8).

Thorne's coiled torsos were a step from the vessel toward a simplified figure that began to incorporate her interest in rhythm and organic growth. *But I always closed them,* Thorne says. *That was a conscious decision related to the idea behind them of contained energy. . . . I made figures because I was examining myself and trying to work out who I am, what I'm doing here, and attempting to make my living being more true to myself than as just a "wage slave.". . . I am very lucky,* Thorne says, *in that I have a very supportive husband who earns enough cash for us to get by without me being under too much pressure to make a living wage . . . but I do hope to do better than just break even. . . . It is important to make what I want and sell everything—that means I can justify what I am doing and that I've made a connection with people.*

Thorne has a passion for gardening. *Being a woman of just 40 and choosing not to have kids, finding satisfaction digging around in the soil, sowing seeds, raising plants,* she hopes to be able to combine her gardening and sculpture, to achieve some sort of balance, possibly predominately gardening during spring and summer and concentrating on her ceramics during autumn and winter, with each feeding off the other.

At the beginning of her professional life in the arts, Thorne is attempting to work out a life pattern that will allow her to develop her own creativity while carrying her share of financial responsibility. As a start on this life scheme, for her master's project Thorne developed a concept that she hopes to market as garden or public sculpture. Her tall assembled works are made up of stamped, glazed clay slabs "strung" on steel rods. These are based on her study of the mathematical researches of

Juliet Thorne and her sculpture, *Fibonacci's Columns.* Ceramic and steel "tablets" impressed with marks relating to growth, fecundity, and renewal. Tallest, 7.7 ft. (2.3 m). Stoneware.

Fibonacci and his theories on number sets that he found repeat themselves throughout nature, as well as on the Golden Section.

Thorne has been studying the technical problems she encountered in creating prototypes for this outdoor sculpture with the thoroughness she applied to building her coiled torsos (3-30, 3-31). She says, *It is clear that I've opened a whole new chapter in my approach to making sculpture during the course of this master's degree project. . . . The process has given me greater scope in showing and marketing the work in the "real" world.* She also feels more confident about the collaborative process she may need to utilize in order to build and market her outdoor work, such as using structural engineers for advice and installation. Thus, although still committed to her personal and inner goals, through her study project Thorne has taken an important step toward those "real life" goals.

BUILDING A COILED FIGURE

3-25 Juliet Thorne, England, devised a technique using continuous spirals of coils that gives her figures rhythm and movement. *This is what gives the spiral form to the whole coiling process,* she says. She rolls the first coil no longer than 2 ft (.6 m), tapering one end. Starting with the tapered coil, Thorne lays it out carefully, shaping the base section. She builds up the form, resting each coil on the one below, without trying to join the coils at this point.

a

b

c

3-26 a When Thorne comes to the end of a coil, she pinches off the end and shapes the end of the next coil to match. Moistening them slightly, she joins them. **b** If the coil is not perfect at this join, she adds a little extra clay and smoothes it on to match the other coils. **c** She continues turning the piece and coiling until it is about 3 in. (77 mm) high. She then lays plastic inside, pressing it gently against the sides; this prevents drying while the outside begins to stiffen. She moistens the top coil slightly.

TIP

Use a turntable and a wooden bat to look at the piece closely. Scrutinize the profile from all angles as you build it up.

3-27   While letting the first section stiffen, Thorne often works on another figure. Once the first figure has stiffened enough to carry the weight of more coils, she removes the plastic and continues building the wall. She closes her figures, but you may wish to leave yours open.

3-28 Thorne says, *I use a small, curved wooden tool to scoop clay upwards on the inside while gently supporting the outside. This ensures a good bonding.*

3-29 As she adds coils, she dampens and scores the ends to join them thoroughly, applying slip to the ends to strengthen the joins.

3-30 Thorne says, *Look carefully at the growing profile of the figure as you go, adjusting where your new coils sit on the one below to achieve the shape you wish.* Each coil is carefully placed to continue the rhythm.

3-31 She coats the finished torso with white slip using a soft brush, giving it a good white base for the glaze. Thorne says, *Adding the glaze holds the piece together more firmly.* (See also Color Plate 7).

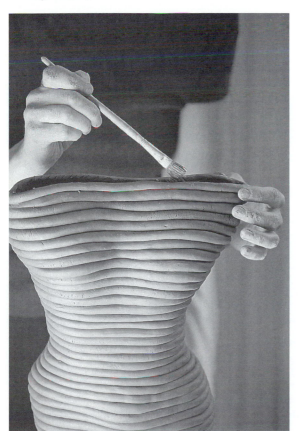

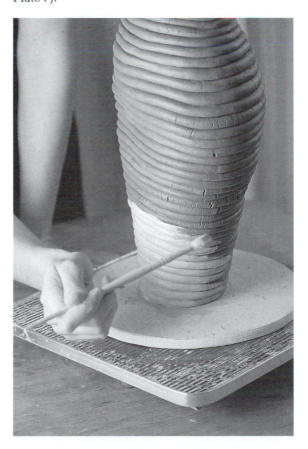

BUILDING A CLOSED POT

3-32   Bryan Gim likes to roll out a number of coils before he starts work. *It speeds up the process so I get continuity, and I need to warm up. By the time I get to my last coil, I'm making good ones.* He cuts a base from a slab, then begins to build on it, melding the first coils carefully to the base.

 TIP

When handrolling coils, apply even pressure. While rolling your fingers forward, spread them out along the coil as you roll.

 TIP

Don't use slip to fill large gaps between dry coils; when the slip shrinks, it will pull away from the coils.

To fill holes or gaps of over 1/16 in. (2 mm), use clay of a similar moisture content, or add more grog to the filler clay to reduce shrinkage.

3-33   First scoring the top coil, Gim then paints each coil with slip in preparation for adding another. *The main problem with coiled pots,* he says, *is not getting the coils attached securely. This is what I call dumb work, but it allows me to take a step back mentally. You need to organize your thoughts.*

3-34 Gim melds the coils thoroughly with a rib. *A lot of times my projects have a concept but don't have a specific finished objective. That comes about during fabrication, but there are so many variables. Serendipitous things happen.*

3-35 Setting each coil slightly inside the one below, he narrows the form into a vase, then decides to make it into a head. He closes it with a plug of clay. *One of the hardest things about clay for me is seeing the end result,* Gim says. *Sometimes you need to know where you are headed. I think sketchbooks are so important.*

3-36 **a** To give some shape to the head, Gim hits the closed pot several times, *for some visual interest. It will make a nice face form.* Gim used a piece of wood, but you may prefer to use a commercial textured or smooth paddle (see drawings). However, it was the indentations from the wood's sharp edge that Gim felt gives interest to the head. **b** A smooth wood paddle is good for shaping a sculpture form. A textured paddle (c) can be useful for overall shaping and adding texture and patterns to a piece.

a

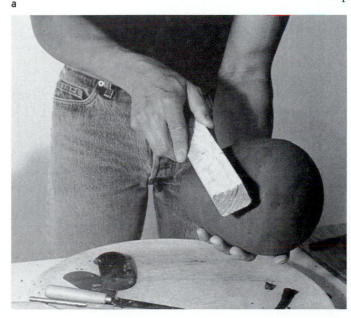

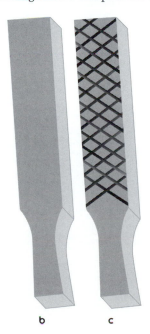

b   c

KEEPING WORK DAMP

If you are unable to complete work on a pot or sculpture in one studio session, in order to continue working on it later you will need to keep it moist. Many school studios have special damp rooms in which work can be kept at the proper damp state for continuation later (3-38). If the studio where you work is not equipped with such a room, then cover your work with plastic sheeting or wrap it in a damp, but not dripping, cotton cloth or damp paper towels, then wrap it in plastic (3-37). The method you choose also depends on how long the piece will stand until your next session, or whether you can come in to the studio to check its condition. If it is forgotten and dries out, it will be difficult to soften it back to working condition without the clay crumbling.

 TIPS

Smooth your work with a rib rather than by adding water.

If you need to dampen your work in progress, flick only a little water onto the clay at a time. Too much water can make the piece collapse.

Don't try to attach dry clay to wet clay or vice versa.

Spray your hands with water and rub them over your piece. This moistens the clay without adding too much water.

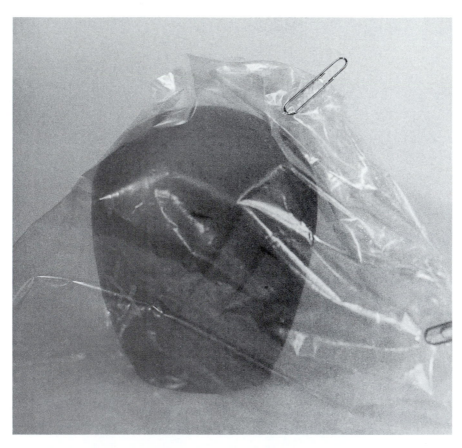

3-37   If you cannot complete a pot or a sculpture in one work session, keep it moist until you can return. Wrap the piece in plastic sheeting or in damp, but not dripping, cotton cloths, then cover it with plastic.

3-38 Peter Coussoulis, manager at the Walnut Creek Civic Arts ceramics studio in California, places an unfired vase on a shelf in the damp room. The room is equipped with an electrically controlled and pressurized steam-generated humidifier. This keeps the pottery and sculpture damp in between class sessions. *Courtesy the City of Walnut Creek, California, Civic Arts Program, Walnut Creek Civic Arts Center. Photo: David Hanney.*

DRYING YOUR WORK

Once you have completed your handbuilt pot or sculpture, you must dry it thoroughly before firing it (3-39 to 3-42).

There may be a drying room or box in your school studio, where the dampness is monitored and the work has a chance to dry slowly. That's the best solution, but if neither of these is available, then tape or staple several sheets of newspaper into a tent shaped to cover the piece, and place it over it (3-39). This lets the work dry slowly, avoiding cracking. For larger pieces, a more elaborate drying tent can be constructed of plastic (3-41).

What is essential is that the clay dry evenly, and the thicker the wall, the longer you should let it dry. The reason for this is that as the water evaporates from the drying clay, its particles will move closer together and the object will shrink. If drying and shrinkage happen too quickly, or if sections dry unevenly, the piece may warp or come apart.

If a dry pot comes apart at the joins, or an arm falls off a piece of sculpture, all is not necessarily lost. It is sometimes possible to moisten the clay at its dry edges with vinegar until the clay is soft enough to score and refasten the sections. Vinegar is a standby for mending broken clay sections or helping attach **leatherhard** pieces. The vinegar's acidity dissolves the edges faster than water does.

As the clay begins its change from the damp malleable state to final fired state (3-42), by the time the ware has become a lighter shade of its damp color, it has reached the **greenware** stage. At this point, the clay will shrink no further until it is fired, but it is especially fragile and should be stored where it will not be damaged before being loaded in the kiln. The theory and practice of firing clay are discussed in Chapter 9.

 TIPS

If your work is drying too fast in a newspaper tent, add more layers. The thicker the walls of the piece, the longer it should stay in the tent.

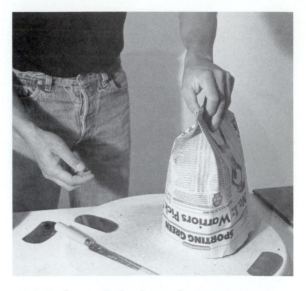

3-39   To dry work slowly, staple newspaper pages together to form a tent. The paper lets the clay breathe, and because the work dries gradually, it is less likely to crack as it shrinks.

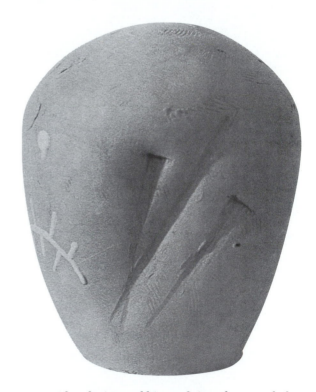

3-40   After drying and bisque firing, the upended, coiled, paddled pot will serve as the basis for one of Gim's sculptured heads. He elaborates their simple forms with layers of colored slips and glazes. Gim says, *Inherent in the coil process is the fact that your pieces come out a little off. That's actually the nice thing. You can't be afraid to lose a piece. You can just do it again. The other thing is you have to roll with the punches. If you are called away and a piece starts drying up, you can't finish it the way you intended. You have to improvise.*

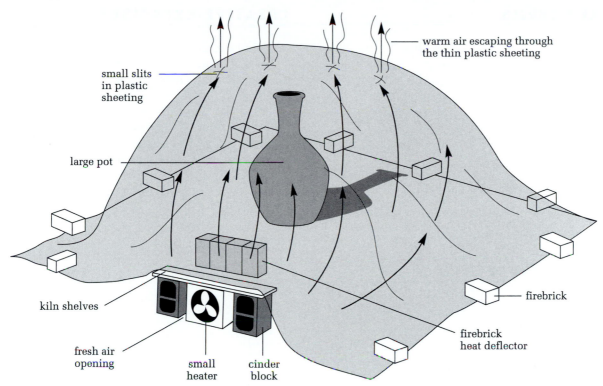

warm air escaping through
the thin plastic sheeting

small slits
in plastic
sheeting

large pot

kiln shelves

fresh air
opening

small
heater

cinder
block

firebrick

firebrick
heat deflector

3-41   Drying tent, useful for predrying large damp
sculptural forms or pots, requires a small electric
heater, bricks, cinder blocks, kiln shelf, and thin
plastic sheeting. Place plastic over the work, heater
between two cinder blocks, and a rectangular kiln
shelf on top of the blocks to keep the plastic away
from the heater. Place four or five bricks as heat
baffles about 15–20 inches (38–51 cm) in front of
the heater. With the heater on, the tent will puff
up with warm air. Four or five slits about 2 inches
(5 cm) cut in the top of the plastic allow steam to
escape.

🏺 **TIP**

When greenware is dry to
the touch, set it in a warm
place with an even heat
source to continue drying.

To check whether your work
is dry, hold it against your
cheek. If the piece feels
cool, there is still moisture
in it, so dry it longer.

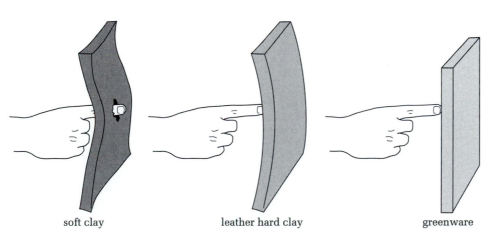

soft clay   leather hard clay   greenware   fired clay

3-42   The four main physical states of clay. 1.) Soft clay; the clay is malleable, easily
joined and best for throwing on the wheel or sculpting. 2.) Leather-hard clay; the clay
has air dried enough to stand on its own, retaining some moisture so slabs can be
joined, or pots trimmed. 3) Greenware: clay is dry, and has shrunk about 5%. Wet clay
can not be attached to greenware. 4) Fired clay; clay has been transformed by heat,
generally shrinking an additional 3–7% when fired to 1915 F. (1046 C).

KEY TERMS

coiling	scoring
modeling	slip
mold	needle tool
burnishing	scoring tool
extruder	leather hard
die	greenware
rib	

CREATIVE EXERCISES

1. Using pinching or coiling, construct a bowl for a special occasion at which you will be a guest or for a meal that you will share with a friend. Shape or decorate your bowl to express your feelings about the occasion or to suggest your friend's personality.
2. Make a coiled or pinched pot or a sculpture that you feel would be an appropriate gift for a public figure. Choose someone you feel has had a significant impact on the world today.

NOTES/SKETCHES

CHAPTER **4**

Slabs and Tiles

Clay slabs are remarkably versatile and can be utilized in many ways. You can use them moist and soft so that they drape and slump, or build with them leather hard (still moist, but stiff enough to hold their shape). They are adaptable to a great variety of work, from vessels to tiles, from constructed sculptures to those with soft, flowing contours. They can create an architectural environment, a slumping lady, or a treasure box. Sometimes you might want the slabs to be rough, carrying the mark of your hand in thick, moist clay. At other times, you may wish to construct a precise geometric form from leather-hard slabs rolled to identical thickness; for yet another piece, you might want to use moist slabs that you can drape into organically shaped pots. Or you may want to pour slip into a mold to make thin slabs that can pick up a delicate carved or stamped image from the mold.

When it comes to constructing vessels or sculpture from slabs, you again have a choice of methods. Some sculpture or vessels are made from just one or two good-sized slabs of

clay; in this case, you may have little difficulty with the one or two joins you need to make. But with other types of slab work that is made of more than one piece, the main technical challenge will be how skillfully you can join the slabs. This means constructing your work so that the joins survive the stress and strain of drying, shrinking, and firing.

You will need to become familiar with the various methods of slab construction, discovering the innate strength of different structural processes. The photographs of the ceramists of varying degrees of experience demonstrating their methods, and their explanations, give you differing answers to the question of when to use a slip and scoring technique. Some ceramists score only the edges; others add slip as a form of "glue"; still others may put an additional coil along the seam for extra reinforcement. We recommend that you score the slabs with a needle tool, nail, or fork and apply slip each time you attach slabs until, ultimately, experience will teach you what construction method works best for you.

HISTORY OF SLABS

The techniques of rolling, pounding, or molding clay into slabs have been utilized for thousands of years, but the use made of the slabs once they were formed has changed over the centuries. For example, in some of the early cultures in western Asia and the Mediterranean—such as Sumeria around 2000 B.C.—slabs provided flat, soft clay surfaces for stamping with symbols and characters that composed the first written words. These record tablets were carefully kept in archive rooms to list palace or temple supplies, to preserve the texts of treaties between rulers, or even to file a potter's glaze recipe.

Ceramists also formed and fired clay slabs into wall, roof, and floor tiles that were used

4-1 Slabs were not often used for sculpture in early cultures, but parts of this warrior made in Japan around A.D. 600 were slab formed. *Haniwa* figures such as this one were placed around the mounded graves of royalty. Late Tumulus period, c. sixth century A.D. *Courtesy Asian Art Museum of San Francisco. The Avery Brundage Collection, B 60 S204.*

4-2 Models of temples, palaces, or houses that were placed in the graves of important persons are the most commonly excavated slab sculpture from early cultures. Some, like this model made in Peru around A.D. 400, give us a clear idea of how buildings looked at that time. Ht. 5¾ in. (14.8 cm). North Coast, Peru. *Courtesy Linden-Museum, Stuttgart, Germany. Photo: Didoni.*

4-3 This tile, glazed in black, yellow, and green, was made in the *cuenca* technique in Spain. When the clay was moist it was stamped with designs, forming indentations that kept the colors separated when the glaze melted in the kiln. Tiles like this one made in Spain were influenced by Arab techniques and designs, so the combined style is called Hispano-Moresque. *Gift of Sarah and Eleanor Hewitt, 1929–17–20. © Cooper-Hewitt National Design Museum, Smithsonian Institution/Art Resource, N.Y.*

4-4 In the nineteenth century, a group of artists in Britain and the United States rebelled against the current industrialism and returned to the past for inspiration in what they called the arts and crafts movement. They frequently depicted natural forms in their work and generally used hand processes. English artist William Frend De Morgan was highly influential in the movement and created many tile installations. *Purchased in memory of Georgiana L. McClellan, 1953–104-4. © Cooper-Hewitt National Design Museum. Smithsonian Institution/Art Resource, N.Y.*

to protect the outer walls of buildings constructed of sun-dried bricks. Then, when potters learned how to make brightly colored glazes, color was added to the walls by facing them with glazed bricks. These also protected the unfired bricks.

Slabs were not often used in early sculpture, but some examples include the Haniwa sculptures in Japan that surrounded mounded tombs (4-1). These were derived from earlier wheel-thrown cylinders. Later potters combined thrown forms with slabs to build sculptures of warriors, horses, and attendants. Some Peruvian grave sculptures of houses, palaces, or temples are also slab built (4-2). Through the centuries, tile makers have continued to hand-form or mold tiles that display many decorative styles for palaces, mosques, or churches (Color Plate 3). In Spain the Arab influence led to a mixed style, called Hispano-Moresque, a specialty of which was richly decorated tiles (4-3). By the time the nineteenth-century arts and crafts revival movement became influential in England and the United States, the tiles

4-5 Painter Paul Gauguin carved this slab-formed vase with **relief** images of Tahitian gods and goddesses. Gauguin created several sculptural clay vessels, working in various potter's shops. Low-fire clay, unglazed. c. 1893–1895. *Courtesy the Museum of Decorative Art, Copenhagen.*

designed by William Frend De Morgan (4-4) harked back to the earlier days of tile design.

In Japan, potter-painters made slab trays with delicate decoration, and at the end of the nineteenth century, a few artists in Europe used slab techniques to build sculptural ceramic vessels (4-5). As the twentieth century progressed, slab vessels and slab plates and vases became more common. Art movements such as cubism and constructivism changed the outlook and methods of some sculptors who no longer modeled in clay, then cast their work in bronze. Instead, they constructed it. This change in technique in turn influenced clay sculptors in the 1950s and 60s to work more directly and freely (5-7). Artists sometimes incorporated slabs into **mixed-media** works or took advantage of the organic forms that soft slabs create.

Sculpted or hand-decorated tiles are still a popular use of slabs, while architectural **installations** incorporating handformed tiles and sculptured slab forms have frequently been commissioned (4-6, Color Plates 9, 21).

4-6 A variety of tile decorating techniques were used by Kary Coke to demonstrate stamped designs and textured and modeled areas by applying damp clay, carving, and incising the leather-hard slabs with a needle tool.

MAKING SLABS

Since slabs can be used in a moist and soft or leather-hard state for pottery or sculpture, choosing which type you need to make depends on your project and the construction method you will utilize. In fact, the moisture content of the slabs has much to do with how you make the slabs and how you work with them once they are formed.

There are a number of ways you can make basic slabs that you can alter as your project dictates. You can sling a chunk of clay down in a sweeping diagonal motion onto a flat, porous surface (4-7) until it stretches out into a slab of uniform thickness. Another way is simply to pound or press the clay onto any absorbent material such as plywood, a plaster wedging table, a **bat** (4-8a), or a canvas-covered surface. Alternatively, you can carefully roll out the clay with a heavy rolling pin or a dowel (4-9). It is possible to cut the slabs to the exact thickness you wish, using strips of wood and a wire (4-10). You can also make slabs with a mold. The mold can be carved or stamped to create decorated surfaces by pressing moist clay or pouring slip into it. This is a good way to reproduce a delicate or detailed design (see Chapter 6, Molds).

Finally, an easy and quick way to produce smooth slabs of consistent thickness is to use a mechanical **slab roller** (4-11).

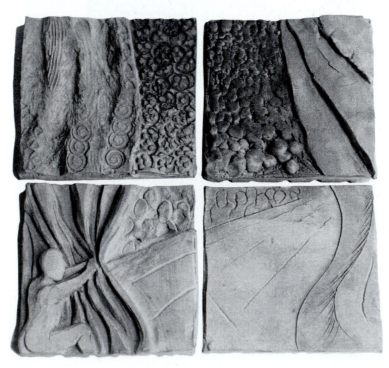

4-7 Throw a chunk of clay down in a sweeping diagonal motion onto a flat, porous surface. Do this two or three times, turn it 90 degrees, and do it again to even out the overall shape of the slab. Continue until the clay stretches out into a slab of uniform thickness.

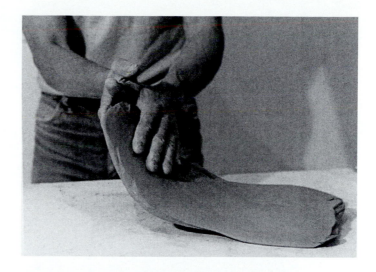

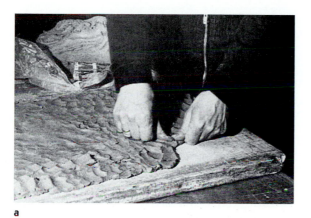

a

b

4-8 Helly Oestreicher, the Netherlands, presses chunks of clay firmly onto a plaster bat to form slabs. **b** She slices off the top layer to smooth the surface.

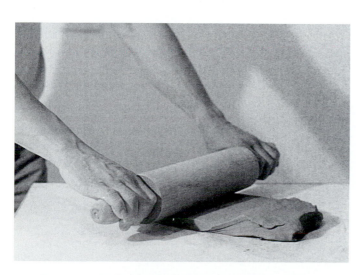

4-9 You can use a kitchen rolling pin to make slabs, but the weight of a heavy, commercial rolling pin will more easily roll out large, dense slabs.

 TIPS

For easiest slab forming, roll clay while it is soft, then let it stiffen before cutting it to shape.

Watch for any air bubbles that may appear as you roll your slabs. Prick bubbles with a needle tool, then smooth the slab with a flexible metal rib.

a   b

4-10 a Here, a thin slab is cut from an already-rolled thick slab. The sticks not only guided the roller and contained the clay while rolling it out, but also help the ceramist see that the slabs end up the same thickness. **b** By removing both of the top sticks and by cutting off a slab with a wire, you can make several thinner slabs of the same thickness.

4-11 A mechanical slab roller quickly makes well-compressed slabs of consistent thickness. It is especially useful for slabs that will be used for building hard-edged forms with stiff clay. *Courtesy the Richmond Art Center Ceramics Studio, Richmond, California. Photo: Carl Duncan.*

BUILDING WITH SLABS

Hardedged Forms

To build hardedged forms, you should make slabs that are smooth and consistent in thickness, using whatever method you prefer. Then dry them to the leather-hard stage so that they will hold their shape while the piece is being constructed. To learn how to join leather-hard slabs, we suggest that you practice with a simple boxlike form or a not-too-tall slab vase.

Hardedged slab forms require extra care in assembling. The stresses on the clay during building, drying, and firing can cause cracks or can separate poorly attached slabs. Scoring, then painting the edges of the slabs with slip mixed to about the consistency of yogurt (4-12, 4-13) is an insurance against cracking. It also helps if you reinforce the joins with a thin coil of added clay (4-14). If the edges become a bit too dry, you can soften them by painting them with ordinary kitchen vinegar. Then score them again and repeat the process, adding more vinegar. Once the edges have softened enough, apply slip and join the slabs.

TIP

Even if slabs seem damp enough to meld together without scoring, until you learn by experience where cracks or separations are most likely to occur during drying and firing, play it safe: Score and paint the edges of all slabs with slip, even if the slabs seem damp enough.

4-12 Larissa Martin demonstrates how she scores the joins and applies the slip to leather-hard slabs. She also scores the join a second time after the slip is applied. She says, *Even if the slabs were moist, I would score and slip coat them.*

Open Box to Sculpture

Once you have learned to make a basic hard-edged form, you can begin to be inventive with your slabs. Larissa Martin (4-13 to 4-15) made an open box form from leather-hard slabs, then developed a large sculpture from several boxes (4-16). In the process, she demonstrates the careful construction method she used to en-sure that the box will fire well and that it preserves the characteristic sharp edges.

 TIP

Use vinegar to moisten too-stiff sections before scoring and attaching them to each other. To help in reattaching broken parts, apply a small amount of vinegar on the edges to be joined. The acid vinegar rapidly penetrates the clay, moistening it so that sections can be scored and rejoined.

To join heavy slabs or stiff clay, paint the edges with a thick mixture of clay and water blended to at least the consistency of yogurt.

For a tight join after scoring and painting the edges of stiffened slabs, slide them back and forth against each other slightly as you press them together.

4-13 To make a slab box, Martin scores the edge of each section where two slabs will be joined, before painting it with slip.

4-14   Martin continues to work around the box, joining the slabs at the corners, reinforcing them with well-melded coils of clay. While she works, she contemplates how she will alter the rectangular form and what she will add to make it into a sculpture. **a** To be sure the slabs will be firmly joined, Martin coats each side with a thick mixture of slip before joining two sections. **b** Before continuing to attach the sections, she test-assembles them to be sure they will fit properly. **c** To strengthen the joins, she rolls a thin coil and places it along the seam, **d** then melds the coil into the seam.

b

a

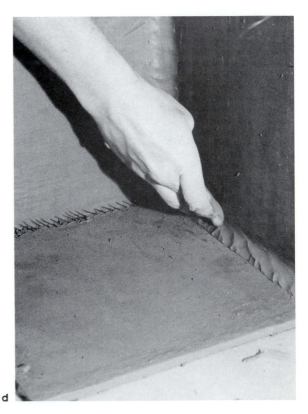

c

TIP

When building hard-edged forms from leather-hard slabs, always score and paint the edges with slip.

d

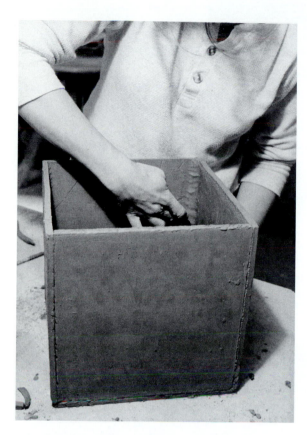

4-15   Martin reinforces the corners by pressing a coil into each joint. For final assembly, the top edge of the box will be scored and slip applied. A leather-hard slab, scored and with slip applied on the perimeter, will be set on the rim, then carefully pressed into place, closing the form. *Courtesy the artist.*

With added confidence, you can now advance to more complex projects and discover how the comparative moistness or stiffness of the slabs affects the type of work you create. You can experiment to see just how much bending and shaping leather-hard slabs will take without cracking or distorting. For example, combinations of stiff and somewhat softer slabs can contrast a hard-edged base with a curved lid for a "treasure box" (4-17 to 4-21; Color Plate 16). Slabs can be adapted to create functional (4-22, 4-23) or nonfunctional vessels, mixed-media constructions, figurative work (4-24, 5-10), or even large installations (Color Plate 25).

4-16   *Untitled,* by Larissa Martin. Instead of turning the box she demonstrated making into a small sculpture, Larissa Martin made an additional set of boxes and crowned them with a tree—possibly a comment on the destruction of forests cut down to make shipping boxes? The work is 67 in. (1.7 m) tall and is built in three sections, glued together with silicone. Martin used ceramic stains to color the surface. *Courtesy the artist.*

4-17 Sara Kotzamani first makes cardboard templates (patterns), then lays them on a slab to cut out the box and lid, taking great care with the corner angles where the seams will be joined.

4-18 With the slab stiff enough to hold its shape, but soft enough to respond to careful bending and shaping, she scores, then paints the corner edges of the box with slip.

4-19 Carefully bending up each corner of the box, aligning and joining the edges, Kosmani then works on the inside, pressing the edges together, compressing and melding the clay with a tool. As she works, she smooths in additional slip as reinforcement.

4-20 She follows the same procedure to make the lid. Taking careful measurements, she then makes a narrow frame to serve as a flange and, after scoring and painting the inside of the box, attaches the flange on which the lid will rest.

4-21 With the box and lid assembled, Kosmani gently manipulates and tools the box to soften its shape, giving it a soft, pillowlike appearance. She also attaches small slabs and decorates them with incised lines, stamped textures, or glazes. (See Color Plate 15.)

4-22   When Gary Holt builds slab vessels, he paints the leatherhard joins with wax-resist compound to keep them from drying too quickly.

4-23   *Vase,* by Ed Persike, constructed with slabs and a wheel-thrown collar. The flowers and butterflies were directly sculpted on the vase surface using a palette knife. Stoneware glazes, fired to cone 6. 11 × 11 × 36 in. (28 × 28 × 91 cm). *Courtesy the artist. Photo: Dr. C. Persike.*

4-24   *Silhouette,* by Elizabeth Roberts, is constructed with slabs and the surface textured using the sgrafitto technique. Low fire underglazes, glazes, and China paint. 3 × 10 × 14 in. (8 × 25 × 36 cm). *Courtesy the artist. Photo Kent Jolly.*

4-25 *Cirque,* by David Shaner. The swelling, hollow form of *Cirque* was created from a soft slab; then Shaner altered it, contrasting organic eruptions with sharp folds and peaks, while the opening allows a glimpse of mystery inside. Stoneware, 22 × 22 × 6 in. (56 × 56 × 15 cm). *Photo: Marshall Noice.*

SOFT SLAB CONSTRUCTION

Used in the soft state, slabs clearly behave quite differently from leather-hard ones. To form organically shaped pots (4-25) or sculpture (4-26, 4-27) from soft slabs, you will generally need to provide a support to help the slabs take and hold the desired shape until they dry enough to retain it on their own. In Chapter 6, Molds, you can learn to make simple plaster molds, but in the meantime, crumpled newspaper shaped into an approximation of the form you wish to build is helpful. A blown-up balloon or a bag of plastic pellets or sand can also serve as a support over which to lay the slabs.

Soft slabs are particularly adaptable to figurative sculpture, since the rounded contours they assume appear almost lifelike. The natural slumping of soft slabs can be exploited to give character to a piece of expressive sculpture or to achieve a sense of lively vitality.

In joining soft, moist slabs, experience will help you decide when you need to score and paint with slip. Some ceramists believe that even if a slab is moist it should be painted and scored before joining. Others feel this is not necessary. Like so many aspects of ceramics, it depends on experience and personal choice. Whatever method you use to join them, it is essential to attach the sections well to ensure that they resist separating as they dry.

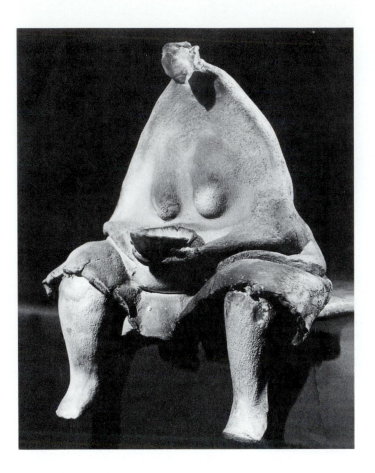

4-26   Lorraine de Castro, Puerto Rico, built her expressive figure, *Doña Dita,* from moist slabs, allowing them to slump as the clay responded to gravity. She rolls her slabs by hand, then models the forms by pushing from underneath. Sculpture mix. Iron, copper, cobalt oxides. *Courtesy the artist.*

4-27   *Mask With Red Mouth,* by Nilsgunnar Zander, Sweden. Zander's direct, strong handling of the moist clay creates a living mask that seems about to speak through its red-glazed mouth. 8 × 6 in. (20 × 15 cm) Porcelain. *Photo: Håkon Johansson.*

4-28 *CDI*, by Jules de Balincourt. A relief wall piece incorporating thrown, altered, and assembled forms. The surface is colored with high-fire slips. It is also a mixed-media piece—the arm of the woman on the right is made of cast glass. Ht. 36 × 43 in. (91 × 109 cm). *Courtesy the artist. Photo: Cida Fukushima.*

4-29 *Distancia*. Sculptor Eduardo Andaluz, Spain, uses slabs for individual wall pieces that he transforms by elaborating the surface with carving, intricate clay additions, and splashed slip. He uses various **oxides** to create muted surface colors that emphasize the enigmatic quality of the works. 14 × 19 in. (23 × 36 cm). *Courtesy the artist. Photo: Leo Marrero.*

TILES

Making Tiles

Tiles are, obviously, a form of slab, whether they are made by hand or by using various devices to speed up production. Historically, tile makers pressed damp clay into some sort of mold—a wooden form or a fired clay mold. Today, handmade tiles may be made by **press molding** or by **slip casting.** To speed up production, you can use a slab roller and cut the tiles using templates to cut around. These methods may be used to create multiple tiles quickly, after which the tiles can be altered by hand in various ways—by stamping, **sprigging,** or carving to create one-of-a-kind pieces (4-28, 4-29, 4-32). (See also Chapter 6.)

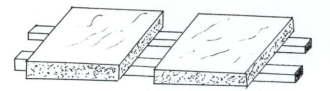

4-30 Setting damp, leather-hard clay tiles on wooden slats will promote even drying and reduce warping or cracking problems.

4-31 Placing damp clay tiles between layers of plaster board (sheet rock) will help to keep them flat as they dry.

Drying Tiles

To avoid having your tiles **warp** as they dry, it is best to leave them to dry untouched on a wooden board or plaster bat. Once they shrink and dry to the point that they no longer stick to the wood or plaster and can be removed easily, you can place them on wooden slats so they will dry evenly in the air (4-30).

Tiles can also be dried on wooden slats or placed between plaster bats (4-31) or pieces of sheetrock. These will absorb the moisture from the clay evenly and keep the tiles from warping. Warping of tiles is also often caused by too-quick drying in the sun or in a dry, windy atmosphere. Under these conditions, where the top of a tile might dry and shrink faster than the undersurface, the whole tile may warp or crack. In addition, the stress on a tile from being peeled from a board or bat too soon, then reflattened, can cause it to warp.

Tiles do not always have to be square. A low relief sculpture can be modeled and carved in one large piece, then cut apart into irregular pieces following the contours of the forms, rather like a jigsaw puzzle. It can then be installed piece by piece on a panel or directly to a wall, and grouted. The artistic possibilities of tiles are almost endless, and once you have learned the basic process, creating a tile work can be a satisfying project.

WALL RELIEFS

One way to create a low-relief wall piece is to roll out or pound an appropriate amount of clay for the size piece you wish to make, being sure to allow for shrinkage, depending on the clay used. Mark Messenger worked in this way to make his *Ready-Made* wall panel (4-32, Color Plate 9). Using this method, your work can be formed on a piece of sheet rock, which will allow the clay to dry evenly and will also decrease warpage as you work on it. Then, once relief modeling, carving, or other surfacing has created the image you want, you can cut the whole piece into smaller tiles and when leather-hard hollow them out at the back. Messenger created a rich surface on his work using low-fire underglazes and glazes. After multiple firings he fastened the tiles to a wooden panel with industrial adhesive for wall mounting.

4-32 Entitled *Ready-Made,* Mark Messenger's slab wall piece was modeled from a single slab of white earthenware clay approximately one to two inches thick. Working with the clay on a piece of sheet rock, he used drawing, carving, modeling, and impressing to develop the image. The slab was then cut into tiles, hollowed out at the back to lighten it, and bisque fired at cone 04. He then surfaced it with underglazes and glazes in layers and fired it twice at cone 05 to achieve the final surface. Earthenware. 3 ft (0.91 m) × 28 in. (711 mm) × 1–2 in. (25 to 51 mm) (See also Color Plate 8) *Courtesy the artist.*

KEY TERMS

relief	press mold
mixed-media	slip casting
installations	sprigging
bat	oxide
mold	warping
slab roller	

CREATIVE EXERCISES

1. Construct a "container for your dreams" from moist or leather-hard slabs in any shape. Its imagery or forms should reflect your daydreams or nighttime dreams. Incise, carve, or apply decoration on the surface, or decorate it with underglaze.

2. Using leather-hard slabs, construct a box for one of your most treasured possessions.

3. Build a model of your dream house or of a public building. The exterior should suggest who you are or what the public building will be used for.

4. Cut a number of slab tiles and decorate them while the clay is damp. Imagine they will be placed around your fireplace or another spot in your home. Use images that depict your special interests.

5. Using thin slabs, cut several small decorative shapes as pendants for special friends. Make each shape represent how you feel about that person. Punch a hole at the top, then glaze and fire the shapes.

NOTES/SKETCHES

CHAPTER 5

Sculpture

Clay sculpture is an exacting art. Sculptor Arthur Gonzalez (5-17 to 5-20, Color Plate 17) explains cogently why he does it:

I find that I make art for three reasons. One is that I find myself enjoying the ability to create something that will reveal to me something new about my nature. Another reason is that I intellectually find the pursuit of communicating in the nonverbal language of visual art extremely important to the human spirit, as history has shown to us. But thirdly and perhaps most importantly, the driving force behind the activity of making art is that I know it is what I can do well in a way no one else can do.

Whether one of those reasons also leads you to clay sculpture, or other concerns are your driving force, the first challenge in creating clay sculpture is to make the material stand up as you work on it. For this necessary support, you may need to use a removable **armature** (5-14). Then you have to learn how to manipulate the pliable clay in order to develop the forms of the sculpture in relation to each other in three dimensions. Placing your work on a banding wheel or a revolving sculpture stand (1-5) makes it easy to turn the sculpture in order to see it from all angles. It is all too easy, if you are unused to working in three dimensions, to forget to turn a piece of sculpture and model it diligently in one area until you are satisfied—then, when you see it from another angle, to discover that the remainder of the piece does not work with the already finished section. This sometimes requires drastic measures—even starting over again.

You also need to understand that moist clay goes through a series of metamorphoses: from its wet and malleable state to a leather-hard material that is still capable of being formed; then shrinking as it dries to a still carvable state; and finally, after firing, becoming so altered that you can change it only by smashing, drilling, grinding, or sawing it.

Thus, you must build your work to survive, constructing it carefully so that the tensions that occur as it dries and is fired do not ruin your piece. Or, if it does come apart, learn from the experience to be more careful of the joins next time.

HISTORY

We don't know just how long people have been forming clay images, but that sculpture, along with utilitarian ware, was an extremely important use of clay very early in human history is clear from the number of small figures that have been found in archeological digs around the world (5-1). Although much of ancient clay sculpture grew out of the desire for ritual or display, one has only to look at some of these images to recognize that their makers also expressed strong personal emotions in the clay.

Many ancient myths—in Egypt and Greece, in the Bible, and in Native American tales, to name a few—tell us that the first human was sculptured from clay by a deity. Other cultures around the world had similar views. The earliest fired clay objects yet found are handsized images of animals and female figures dug up from a hut site dating from about 12,000 to 25,000 years ago when ice covered much of Europe. Since these early sculptures were formed and fired, generations of clay sculptors

5-1 Early in the history of Egypt, an artist used fingers and a hand tool to create an expressive small sculpture. It was probably an offering to a deity, perhaps for fertility, or from a mother requesting health for a sick child. Pre-dynastic Egypt (before 3000 B.C.). *Copyright British Museum.*

5-2 Seated clay figures do not present the construction problem that standing figures do because the bench or chair gives adequate support. This painted Etruscan portrait figure may represent a member of the family in whose tomb it was found. Seventh century B.C. *Copyright British Museum.*

have dealt either realistically or expressively with the basic concerns or spiritual searching of human beings.

Although there were clay sculptors in the Etruscan period (c. 500–100 B.C.) in what is now Italy (5-2) and in the Benin court in Africa (5-3), and a few figure sculptors in the fifteenth, sixteenth, and seventeenth centuries in Europe who created fired clay sculpture (5-4 to 5-6), in general, Renaissance sculptors used the material to model sketches or to make full-scale models of figures from which they made molds in order to cast the figures in bronze. This tradition became the academic standard in Western countries, and it was in parts of Africa, China, Japan, and certain areas of the Americas and India that clay remained an honored medium on its own.

5-3 In the independent African kingdom of Benin (mid-twelfth to late-nineteenth centuries), art was centered on the royal court and its ceremonies. Terra-cotta portraits like this may have been originals for bronze portraits placed on the royal ancestral altars, or commissioned by nobles for their own less elaborate altars. Terra-cotta, Benin. Ht. 10½ in. (26.4 cm). *The Field Museum, Chicago. Neg. #A99506.*

5-4 In Renaissance Italy, in areas where good carving stone was rare, ceramic was used instead of marble. This painted, but unglazed terra-cotta *Madonna* sculpted by Niccolo Dell' Arca has remained in place on the facade of the Palazzo del Comune (City Hall) in Bologna since he completed it in 1492.

5-5 Italian sculptor Giovanni Lorenzo Bernini (1598–1680) formed this clay sketch (or *maquette*) with spontaneous gestures, then fired it to permanence. Ht. 11¼ in. (26 cm). *Courtesy of the Fogg Art Museum, Harvard University Art Museums, and Alpheus Hyatt and Friends of the Fogg Art Museum Funds.*

5-6 Antonio Rosellino (1427–1479) worked in Italy and England. His *Virgin and Laughing Child* probably was sculpted as a model for a larger work. The marks of the sculptor's tools are still fresh on the folds of the robe, and his fingerprints can be seen in the hollow interior through an opening in the back. Terra-cotta. Ht. 19 in. (48 cm). © *V & A Picture Library.*

RECENT HISTORY

For many years after the Greek and Roman periods in Europe, clay as a sculptural material was used primarily for sketches and/or for full-sized originals from which molds were made for carving in marble or casting in metal. In other areas, clay continued to be an acceptable material for clay sculpture and was used in India, China, Africa, and indigenous American cultures for important ritual objects and architectural decorations. No line was drawn between the potter and the sculptor.

During the Renaissance period in Europe, a few sculptors created portrait busts with the material, painting them in realistic colors,

and a few sculptors working in the 1940s created large pieces in clay. During the late 1950s and early 1960s a number of potters began to use clay as a sculptural medium, and the interest in polychrome sculpture led many of them to glaze or paint work. The question of clay as art material versus craft material engaged critics, while many art galleries were slow to accept work in glazed clay. The material continued, however, to appeal to artists with differing approaches, such as John Mason, who, in the 1960s created large abstract sculptures enhanced with ceramic glazes (5-7),

5-7 *Cross Form,* by John Mason. Mason was influenced by the abstract expressionism movement in painting and sculpture in the 1950s and 1960s. Translating his response to that movement, he assembled thickly cut slabs and massive forms and glazed them, achieving new images. Such massive work requires lengthy drying and slow firing. 1963. Glazed stoneware. Ht. 7½ ft (2.3 m). *John Mason, American, b. 1927, Cross Form, ceramic, 1962, 161.3 × 132 × 91.4 cm. Gift of the Ford Foundation, 1964. 71, photograph © 1996, The Art Institute of Chicago. All Rights Reserved.*

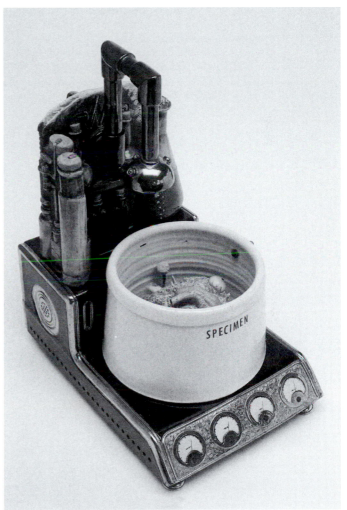

5-8 *Specimen Bowl,* by Clayton Bailey. One of Bailey's influential pieces (1978) that, he says, *are mechanical inventions that 'create life out of mud.'* In this mixed media sculpture he says, *the creature is bubbling and wheezing in a bowl of water. It is self-illuminated, and has realistic laboratory apparatus attached to the bowl for life support. It provides further proof that the artist can create life from mud.* Low-fire and stoneware clay, luster, china paint, glass eye, water, sound, movement. 14 in. (36 cm) × 24 in. (62 cm) × 24 in. (62 cm). *Courtesy the artist.*

and Clayton Bailey, whose narrative style made use of glazed ceramic, water, sound, and movement to create enigmatic images (5-8).

A new approach that made fired clay an accepted sculptural medium like any other occurred only comparatively recently in the 1950s and 1960s in the United States and in Italy (5-7, 5-8; Color Plate 7). Sculpture today has taken many new directions, and sculptors may create their work using computer technology or deal with it as a concept rather than a product. These developments, which affected sculptors in many media, have also influenced clay sculptors who have incorporated mixed media into their work (5-9, 5-10) or display their work as installations (5-9, 5-29 to 5-31; Color Plate 25). At the same time, many clay sculptors continue to express human emotions and comment on social relationships or ethnic issues, and the human figure is prominent in their work.

5-9 *Emblemas,* by Angel Garraza, Spain. Garazza created this work as an opening project for the European Ceramics Work Center, 's-Hertogenbosch, the Netherlands. To make the large circular form, he attached strips of foam pipe insulation to a plywood board, then made a plaster mold from the pipe insulation attached to the wood. He then pressed out the final shape from the plaster mold. Diam. 35 in. (90 cm). Small sections, 30 × 25 × 10 in. (12 × 10 × 4 cm). *Collection, Museum Het Kruithuis, the Netherlands. Photo: Peer van der Kruis, courtesy the European Ceramics Work Center.*

a

5-10   **a** *Jantje,* by Marijke van Vlaardingen, the
Netherlands. Her flying horse was formed from
molded and handformed slabs. **b** Van Vlaardingen
builds one of her figures with slabs. After forming
each section in molds or by handmodeling, she
assembles the parts. **a** *Photo: Kent Marshall. All rights
reserved.* **b** *Courtesy the artist.*

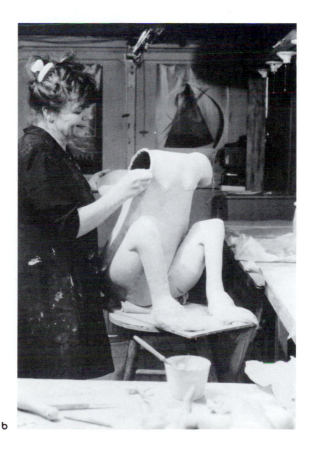

b

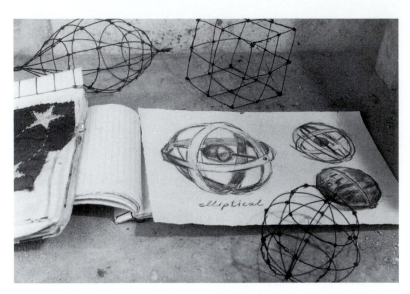

5-11   While working on a series of spherical sculptures, Michelle Kern uses her sketchbooks and large drawings to work out her ideas. Her wire constructions were developed as three-dimensional drawings. *Right now,* she says, *it is enough for me to collect these things into notebooks, and then to try to do work that mirrors this private experience and revelation of a secret cosmology. . . .*

5-12   Kern dry-brushing slip onto one of her sculptures. *I borrow heavily from writings and images of historical astronomy from European and Middle Eastern systems.*

RELIEF SCULPTURE

The term **relief** applies to sculptured works on a flat surface in which the forms are raised only slightly from the flat background—called **low relief**, or **bas relief**—or it can refer to a sculpture whose full contours are almost detached from the background, that is, **high relief.** Most relief falls somewhere in between those two extremes (5-4). From a technical point of view, it is somewhat easier to develop a sculpture in relief than in full round because you do not have the problem of making the moist clay stand up. On the other hand, it is probably aesthetically a more difficult problem to give life to relief sculpture because the light cannot illuminate it in three dimensions. Mark Messenger (4-32, Color Plate 9) used deep carving in his wall relief to produce a play of light and shade across the figures, giving them the appearance of three-dimensions although they are actually in relief.

SCULPTURE-IN-THE-ROUND

From the Ice Age to the present day, sculptors around the world have modeled figures in small, handheld sizes (5-1), but making large, freestanding clay sculptures presents a number of other technical and aesthetic challenges (5-17 to 5-27). When building freestanding sculpture, you must be aware of the importance of carrying the eye fully around the forms of the sculpture. You must also realize the different impressions that static forms and active, billowy forms, sharp jagged-edged forms, or soft rounded contours create in the viewer, and use them as a source of expression. These considerations, as well as the technical ones, call for care and concentration, but they also challenge you to achieve expression of your ideas, bringing you satisfaction when your work is completed.

SKETCHING AND CLAY

Sketching can help you clarify your ideas for sculptures, whether you use it to visualize how a particular form will look (5-11) or to figure out how to support and build a sculpture (5-12). Drawing can help you learn to pay attention to forms in space and suggest how to use them in a visually pleasing or expressive manner. Through sketching what you see around you, whether in a city street or in nature, you can capture fleeting impressions, gestures, and forms that later may be a source of ideas for your sculpture. Use your sketchbook also as a scrapbook to jot down thoughts and to keep photographs, pressed leaves, magazine clippings—anything that may inspire you.

One of the great things about clay is that almost anyone can work in it—even if you are legally blind, you can still use the medium. Your hands will probably already be more sensitive than those of fully sighted persons, and instead of drawing in a sketchbook, you can work out your ideas in small clay sketches, called **maquettes** (5-5), creating works that spontaneously capture your emotions or perceptions. Because of the direct relationship of the maker's hands with clay, these quickly sculpted sketches are intimate expressions of the artist's feelings. Those that have been preserved from the past can give us insight into the creative processes of some of the most noted sculptors, from inception of idea to final form.

TOOLS

Hands as Tools

In Chapter 3, Handbuilding, we spoke of the importance of your hands as tools. This is equally true, or even more so, in sculpture. Nevertheless, there are certain tools that will help you realize your concept in clay. Any of the tools illustrated here (5-13) or in other chapters can be used for clay sculpture. In addition, found objects or household implements can make good tools, either used as is or adapted to your particular needs. If you are a whittler, you can make your own tools from wood, designing them to perform particular tasks. Excellent tools can also be cut from stiff plastic, such as gallon milk jugs. Often a tool you have made yourself will turn out to be a favorite because it is specifically designed for the way *you* work.

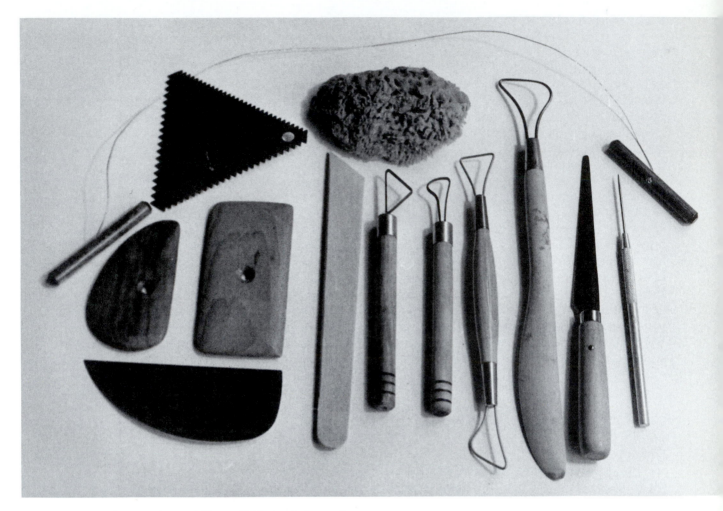

5-13 Some commercially available tools for sculpture. Left: Various types of ribs for smoothing or scoring. Middle: Wooden tool and four sizes and types of loop tools. Right: Fettling knife and needle tool. Top: Sponge, and wire for removing work from the bat.

ARMATURES

An armature (5-14) is used to help support the clay as you build it up into a solid sculpture with the intention of hollowing it out before firing or when you build a hollow form with coils or by pinching. With care, it is possible to build hollow without an armature (5-15) but often some type of support is necessary. Standing figures and attenuated forms especially need supports to keep the clay from slumping or totally collapsing as you work. Wooden dowels, pipes, rolled newspapers, and mailing tubes covered with foam that will compress as the clay stiffens or shrinks will all work well (5-16). Sometimes, rolls or chunks of clay will prove useful as supports while the clay stiffens.

b

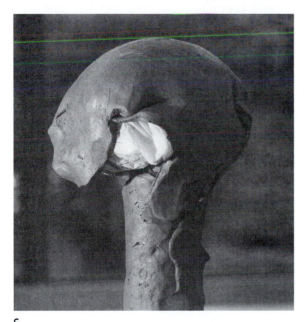

c

5-14 For armatures, use what you find around the house. **a** A cardboard mailing tube, covered with foam and plastic, makes slipping the work off easy and supports vertical forms until the clay stiffens. **b** Dowels inserted in a wooden base and wrapped with crinkled newspaper hold up tall, slender shapes. **c** A bag of plastic pellets, over which the slab will stiffen into a head shape, waits for features to be added.

As you can see in these photographs, and in "Building Solid" (pages 74–76), you can use a variety of materials and methods to support the clay when the project calls for you to do so. Ingenuity is important at this point: The armature material must be stiff and strong enough to support the clay and yet easy to remove.

For hollow heads or other small pieces, supports can be made from crumpled newspapers, balloons, bags of plastic pellets, or shredded foam. Clay can be formed over the supports in coils, pinched-out sections, or slabs. You will soon discover at what point you can remove the support and what particular material works best to support your own project.

69

5-15 *Reborn,* by Chukes, was coil-built hollow. Solid coils form the hair. The facial features were carefully modeled and smoothed to a silky skin texture, contrasting with the strong hands and arms that surround and support the sculpture. Ht. 16 in. (41 cm).

5-16 Armatures to support figures, busts, tubes, vessels, or sculpture can be made with wooden dowels, broom handles, metal or plastic pipes with flanges, soft aluminum wire, bamboo screws, or plastic peanuts in a bag tied to a stick. These supports can be mounted on boards w/screws, metal angles, or nails.

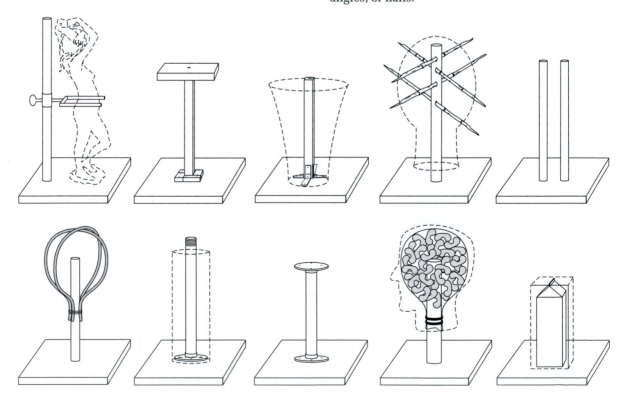

BUILDING HOLLOW

You can make a hollow sculpture without an armature by pinching or coiling up the walls of your forms (5-17 to 5-21; Color Plate 8). This takes patience, but it can be amazing to see how large a sculpture can be built using this process. It is a structurally sound way to work, adaptable to sculptures of different sizes. Frequently you will need to wait until you are sure the lower sections have stiffened sufficiently to support the additional slabs, pinches, or coils of clay you need to add: The method also allows you to develop complex images from simple beginnings. For example, you can start out with a basic coiled or pinched pot, form and shape it into a head, then alter it to develop the detail and nuances of the face. You can also form sections on the wheel and alter them into sculptural forms.

Another way to work hollow is to shape slabs over crumpled paper or make specifically shaped plaster molds as shown in Chapter 6, Molds. Using a different method, Arthur Gonzalez built a head with coils, then transferred the hollow head to his hand, and worked on it by pushing out the features from inside. As the features developed, he modeled and refined them. When the head, neck, and shoulders were finished, he assembled and then fired them. If you want to build a very large hollow sculpture, fit it into the kiln, and fire it, you may have to either construct it in sections or cut it into sections before drying it in order to fire it. One important point to remember when building hollow is to keep the walls of all sections consistent in thickness.

If you fire the sections separately, you can attach them with epoxy glue after firing. Assembling sculpture after firing gives you the freedom to make the entire large work at once; then, if the kiln is not large enough to fire the entire piece at one firing, you can cut it into sections and reconstruct it later.

5-17 Arthur Gonzalez, U.S.A., likes working on his studio floor. Once the shoulders and the neck opening (left) have stiffened sufficiently, he will elongate the neck with more coils. When fired, it will fit into and support the hollow head. This wall sculpture involves engineering a wooden framework and a flange on the sculpture to attach the pieces to the wall (Color Plate 16).

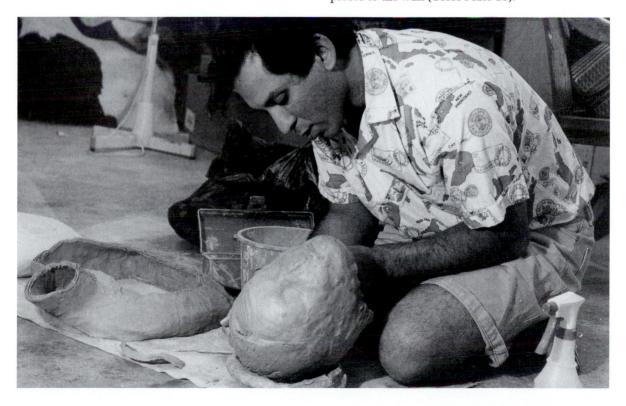

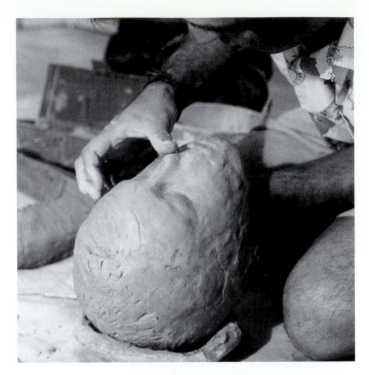

5-18 Gonzalez softened the clay surface by painting it with thick slip before pushing out the features from inside. As he models, the young woman's face comes to life in the clay. Watching a talented sculptor bring this face to life, it is easy to understand early myths that told how a god or goddess formed the first human from clay.

5-19 Using a needle tool, Gonzalez opens the eyes. Note the bisque-fired mold in which the head rests while he works. This gives the head more support than if it was held in his hand, while preserving its rounded contours.

5-20 The artist was surprised by the skeptical personality that emerged. Once the piece is thoroughly dry, he will bisque-fire it and use colored slips and stains to enhance it.

 TIP

It is important to keep one hand inside the head to push out. This eliminates the need to add too much clay to the outer surface, avoiding the possibility of the added clay popping off in firing.

TIP

Be conscious of eye alignment, basing it on the first eye you model.

TIP

Gonzalez says, "In this process, it's important to hold the head up every so often so you can see what's happening with the form.

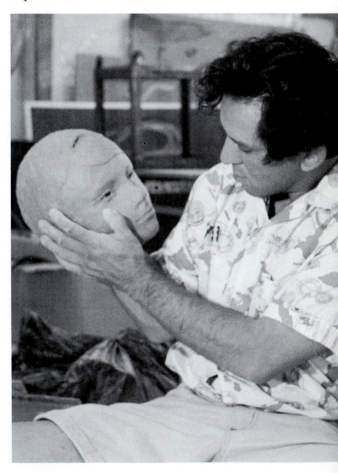

5-21 The thoughtful pose of *Tamara I,* by Peter Schifrin, is expressed by the strength of his direct modeling of the clay. Slab-built stoneware clay, fired to cone 02, and decorated with various non-fired paints, lacquers, metal powders, and whiting. 19 × 11 × 10 in. (48 × 28 × 25 cm). *Courtesy the artist.*

BUILDING SOLID

Since moist clay cannot support much weight without an armature, it is difficult to build a solid standing clay figure, or any tall clay form that stands on a narrow base, without an armature. Even if you manage to get it to stand up, you will find that the clay will want to slump in response to gravity. To avoid this, a pipe, screwed into a flange, which is in turn screwed onto a wooden base, makes an excellent armature that can be pulled out for hollowing before the piece dries. Alternatively, you can make **press molds** of the piece (Chapter 6) and use them to shape forms to be reassembled. Or you can cut apart and hollow out the sculpture, then reassemble it with slip and scoring.

Sara Floor (5-22 to 5-27) made her figure's solid legs sturdy and, for support, used two pipes inserted into the clay without attaching them to a wooden base. She then built the sculpture around these supports, and when the clay became firm yet still damp she was able to pull out the pipes, cut the figure in half, and hollow out the torso and legs.

It is clear from the photographs in this chapter that there are a number of ways to work out the problems presented by the response of clay to gravity. Each piece you make will probably present its own challenge, and you will learn to adapt armatures to each situation. Then, after completion, follow the hints on drying your work in Chapter 3, and you will be able to fire it.

5-22 Sara Floor contemplates the figure that will eventually become her *Pink Venus;* she has already chosen the bright pink glaze she will use on it.

5-23 Floor cuts the leather-hard figure at the waist with a wire and needle tool. Note the pipe support sticking out through the shoulder. *Pink Venus's* legs and feet are sturdy enough for her to stand alone without the pipe being attached to a flange and board. A more attenuated or fragile figure would need greater support.

5-24   a Floor carefully lifts the upper section of *Pink Venus* off the pipe supports that show at the waistline as well as at the shoulder. **b** It takes a careful, strong pull to remove the second pipe without damaging the lower section.

5-25   To hollow out the torso and the legs, Floor supports the sculpture sections on foam rubber, carving out the excess clay with a ribbon tool, making sure to leave walls thick enough to support the weight of the torso.

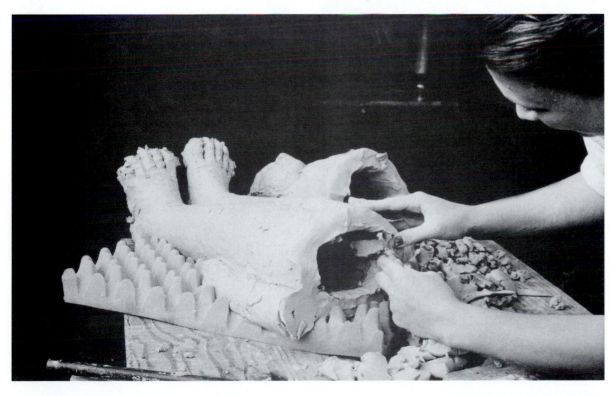

5-26 a Floor deeply scores both parts of the cut sections. **b** She then smears the joint thoroughly with thick slip before reattaching the sections.

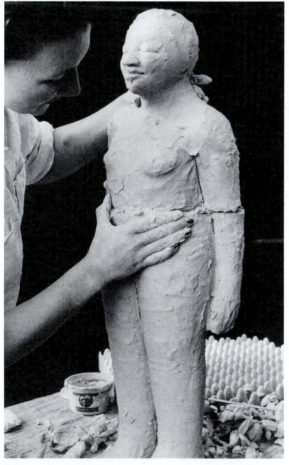
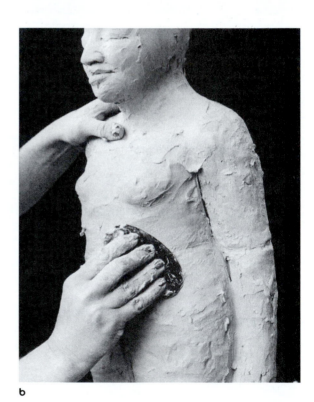

5-27 a Imperturbable, *Pink Venus* submits to the reassembling process. Floor presses the two parts together firmly to make a good join. **b** She then presses more slip into the join with a **rib**, compressing the clay and smoothing the surface before bisque firing and glazing.

MIXED MEDIA AND INSTALLATIONS

In ceramics, a mixed-media work can be either a pot or a sculpture that incorporates glass, metal, wood, paint, paper, textiles, video, sound or light, or any other material you wish to use. We tend to think of mixed-media works as a recent development, but in various cultures throughout the world, clay sculptures and vessels have long been enhanced with feathers, shells, and other materials attached after firing.

Mixed media widens the opportunities for today's clay artists who make use of a variety of materials or replicate them in clay. Even if you do not have facilities for forming metal and firing it into your work (this requires special care in firing), you can still plan to add materials after firing by correctly placing the necessary fittings or holes for their insertion as you sculpt.

Margaret Realica (5-28) constructs most of her sculpture from porcelain slabs that she throws on the wheel, then cuts open, rolls out, and shapes over armatures. This process, she says, ensures that the slabs warp less than conventionally made slabs. Although steel and brass rods and Plexiglas also form part of her assembled sculptures, many of the apparently metal elements such as nuts, rods, and screws are actually porcelain. Realica also impresses computer parts or metal objects into the clay to create texture or transfer lettering. She derives many of her works from deconstruction of the elements of tea-making, including swollen tea bags of glorious color. She then reassembles the parts into "tea pots"—a reference back to her years of making functional teapots. She says, *The machine and its components, the pot, and the concept of tea and tea-making are the root of my current work.* The work is glazed with rich color, often with a metallic sheen, furthering the illusionary quality of the sculpture.

NEW CONCEPTS

Greg Roberts (Color Plate 18) works with honeycomb ceramics—a material designed to filter particles in the air in cars and smokestacks. Roberts says his works comment on the *work*

of agricultural geneticists, whose work can be as benign as generating a redder rose, or as pernicious as creating crops that require licensing agreements from farmers and make it illegal to save or reuse seed.

On the other hand, you can use clay in a more conceptual manner as did Paul Astbury in his moist clay works (5-29) in which he dealt with utilitarian household ceramics in a new way. Astbury's many drawings of everyday domestic objects show the cups and teapots almost disappearing into a dark background. Expanding on this exploration of the theme, in his installation of objects sealed in plastic boxes, the damp clay breathes and changes; at times the moisture causes it to collapse completely into the surrounding clay. At

5-28 *The Gas Main and The Apricot Tree,* by Margaret Realica. Realica's sculpture gives the appearance of assembled mixed-media work, but on closer examination, it is seen as largely constructed of porcelain—except for some bronze rods and Plexiglas. White, opaque, and gloss high-fire glazes, fired to cone 7, then airbrushed with multiple layers of metallic lusters. 13 × 8 × 4 in. (33 × 20 × 10 cm). *Courtesy the artist. Photo: Richard Sargent, Sixth St. Studio, San Francisco.*

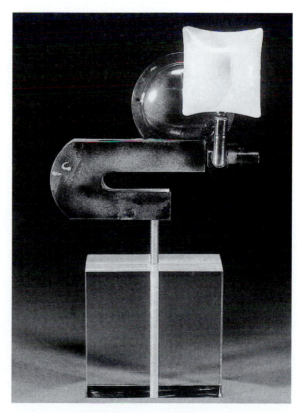

5-29 Part of a gallery installation of cups, teapots, and figurines displayed in sealed boxes. Paul Astbury, England, reexplores the basic material of ceramics by encasing domestic ware in sealed plastic boxes. The damp clay has a life of its own, breathing and reabsorbing the moisture, then releasing it to coat the plastic box so that the object almost disappears. *Courtesy the artist. Photo: Tim Fieldstead.*

5-30 *Support,* by Juan Granados. Granados says, *I have worked the land in various parts of the country and have harvested many types of crops and produce. All of this is part of me, and I have enjoyed celebrating these experiences of cultivation. . . . My work is a mirror of a past that I constantly reconstruct for visions of the future.* Earthenware, 29 × 19 × 11 in. (74 × 48 × 28 cm). Bisque fired at 04. Glazed at cone 06–05, oxidation. Highly concentrated copper to achieve the leadlike glaze. *Photo: Jon Q. Thompson.*

other times the dampness is reabsorbed back into the surrounding clay so that no moisture beads appear on the surface of the object. Under other atmospheric conditions, the moisture collects on the plastic, creating fog or drops of moisture that slide down the window. Therefore, Astbury, who has for many years made mixed-media sculptures, has now turned to reexploring the basic material of ceramics—damp clay.

INSTALLATIONS

In addition, once installations became popular in the art world, clay artists found the idea intriguing because it meant they had a broader scope for their skills. Now, by planning an installation, a ceramist can express ideas that would be difficult to develop in single pieces of sculpture. Thus, the extent of clay's expressiveness can be expanded. Juan Granados (5-30) says that his work in clay connects to his experiences of working with the land. *Now,* he says, *I enjoy cultivating clay as a means of expressing ideas connected with human sustainability.* Granados develops his individual wall pieces and his installations, Color Plate 12, by drawing on his background as the child of migrant agricultural workers. To build his sculptures and installations, he uses a paper support, similar in construction to Mexican piñatas, and also uses balloons as supports; if he can't find the correct shape of balloon, he uses a few taped together. After the clay has stiffened sufficiently to be removed, Granados reinforces the piece with a second layer of clay. He then refines the surface with ribs made from coffee-can lids. Using newspaper to absorb the moisture, he dries the pieces carefully before firing.

5-31 Lourdan Kimbrell created an installation combining clay, feathers, rocks, and sand to remind us what our demands for oil can do to wild creatures. *Courtesy the artist.*

Potters and sculptors are generally particularly concerned about environmental issues, perhaps due to working in close contact with earth materials. Lourdan Kimbrell, for example, uses both mixed media and the installation format to remind us of the impact our consumer society has on wildlife (5-31).

KEY TERMS

armature	maquette
relief	press mold
low relief	mixed media
bas relief	installation
high relief	

CREATIVE EXERCISES

1. Use pinching, coiling, or slab-building techniques to make a monument to yourself that incorporates some aspect of your personality or life experience for which you would like your friends and family to remember you.
2. Using moist slabs combined with coils, sculpt a small hollow figure portraying yourself or someone close to you at an important moment in life. Build the body over a pipe or rolled paper, and form the head over a bag of plastic pellets or crumpled newspaper.
3. Throw three forms in various sizes on the wheel. Combine these with coiled or pinched forms to build a sculpture that expresses intense emotion.

NOTES/SKETCHES

CHAPTER 6

Molds

The clay-forming techniques you have explored so far have used only your hands—or tools in your hands—to shape the clay. The process of using molds, however, changes that direct connection between your hands and the material.

The ability to form clay quickly by using molds makes the process popular, while the fact that you can use a mold to make copies of your original saves work and time when making multiples. For example, Michelle Kern used a mold to reproduce her clay spheres (5-12), avoiding the time-consuming process of sculpting each one by hand.

In addition, using a mold process allows you to form a solid original and then make a hollow cast of it that is light, structurally strong, and capable of being fired safely. You can also make a mold from your original work, make several casts from it, then alter and enhance each of the multiples.

Molds can be used to form clay by pressing lumps of it into a **press mold** or **bisque mold**

(6-1, 6-2, 6-8, 6-9), by laying slabs over a **hump mold,** by placing slabs carefully in a **drape mold,** or by pouring semiliquid clay into a **slip-casting mold** (6-3, 6-19 to 6-25; Color Plate 18). A hump mold can be a ready-made commercial plaster mold (6-5), a kitchen bowl with plastic sheeting over it (6-6), crumpled newspaper, or even a rock—any form *over* which you can place wads, coils, or slabs of clay and let the clay stiffen until it holds its shape without slumping.

Although most press molds are made of plaster, any open form you can find that does not have **undercutting** will allow you to make a replica by pressing the clay *into* it.

An absorbent mold made of casting plaster or high-grade pottery plaster, however, has the advantage of drawing the moisture out of the clay quickly. The absorbency of the plaster and resulting shrinkage of the clay wall allow easy separation of the cast from the mold. A plaster mold that is thoroughly dry will form a wall quickly, while a damp mold will require more time.

HISTORY

For several thousand years, potters and sculptors have adapted the use of molds to a variety of ceramic applications. Probably the first mold was a hump mold—perhaps a river-smoothed rock over which someone formed a container. In many early cultures where domestic pottery was generally formed with rounded bases, potters used the base of a broken pot or a specially made terra-cotta mold in which they placed the clay as they began to shape a pot (3-20).

The need for votive offerings to be presented to deities led to the use of porous terra-cotta molds to press-cast large numbers of low-relief figurines quickly (6-1). In Peru, within the first millennium A.D., press molds were used to make portrait vessels from mold-made sections that were joined after forming (8-4). Press molds were also used in various cultures in Mesoamerica, during the same period. There, potters press-molded small, appliqué shapes and used them to cover the surfaces of large ritual urns and incense burners (6-2).

In ceramics workshops in Europe and the United States, multipart plaster molds were used to cast innumerable decorative ceramic figurines (6-3). Around the world, potters have used various types of molds to form slabs into platters or low dishes (6-4).

6-1 This half-round bodhisattva figure was cast in a porous terra-cotta press mold. A one-part mold could release the amount of relief on this figure, but to cast a full-round sculpture would require a multipart mold. India, late third to fifth century A.D. © V & A Picture Library.

6-2 Incense burner from Teotihuacán Valley of Mexico, decorated with mold-formed appliqué badges that identify the figure on the lid as Quetzalcoatl. c. A.D. 800. Ht. 24¼ (62 cm). *Copyright © Denver Art Museum, Denver, Colorado.*

6-3 Slip-cast decorative human and animal figurines were produced in great quantity in Europe and the United States in the eighteenth and nineteenth centuries. Although the main figure was cast in a mold, often details like the curly hair on this stoneware poodle were applied after casting. 1849 to 1858. Ht. 8½ in. (22 cm). *Courtesy the Brooklyn Museum, H. Randolph Lever Fund. Acc. #74.19.3.*

6-4 Japanese painter and calligrapher Kitaoji Rosanjin (1883–1959) was the owner of a restaurant for which he made pottery. This mold-formed slab platter by Rosanjin was fired in the kilns of Bizen in Okayama Prefecture, Japan. *Kitaoji Rosanjin, Japanese, 1883–1959, Chop Dish with Moon and Grasses, Bizen Ware, n.d., 4.8 × 25 × 45.2 cm. Gift of Miss Margaret O. Gentles, 169.697, photograph © 2000. The Art Institute of Chicago. All rights reserved.*

6-5 Multiple plates and shallow bowls can be shaped over a plaster hump mold, which will rapidly absorb the moisture. The slab should be damp and firm to the touch. A foot formed from a coil can be attached to the bottom of the slab while the leather-hard plate or bowl is on the mold. Commercially made molds in various sizes and shapes can be bought in ceramics supply stores.

HUMP MOLDS

Almost any form that can support moist clay can be used as a hump mold if it has no undercutting (6-5 to 6-7). In addition to using ready-made plaster hump molds, you can place slabs of clay over a household object like a mixing bowl (6-6) covered with thin plastic sheeting, but you must remove the clay before it dries, shrinks, and cracks. If your slabs are not too heavy, you can use bundled newspapers, plastic pellets, shredded foam in plastic bags (5-14c), or even a balloon as molds or supports that will yield as the clay shrinks. These can be pulled out after the clay stiffens, before firing.

The human body has also been used as a hump mold, as in the Italian Renaissance when sections of almost-life-size terra-cotta figures were sometimes shaped over parts of the human body—a method still in use by some sculptors.

6-7 Ernst Haüsermann, Switzerland, formed this ash-glazed bowl over a large plaster hump mold, shaping it by slapping the clay with his palms. Ht. 9½ in. (24 cm). Length 21 in. (53 cm). *Courtesy the artist.*

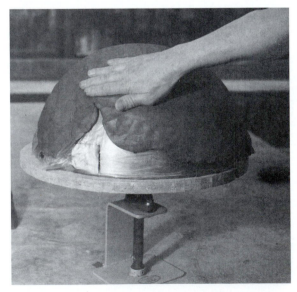

6-6 Look for objects like this large salad bowl that you can use as hump molds. Covering the object with a thin layer of foam or several layers of newspaper will allow the clay to shrink as it stiffens.

 TIP

Remove the clay form from a hump mold when it holds its shape yet is still slightly pliable and damp. This ensures release of the clay before it shrinks and cracks on the rigid mold.

Plate 1
Mayan potters made cylindrical vessels on which
court and temple scenes were painted. This vessel
shows the ritual ball game played throughout
Mesoamerica. A.D. 650–800. Found at the Ik
Emblem Glyph site. Ceramic with slip. 8 1/16 in. ×
6 1/4 in. (20.3 × 15.9 cm). *Courtesy Dallas Art Museum, gift
of Patsy R. and Raymond D. Masher. 1983.148. Photo © 2000,
Dallas Museum of Art*

Plate 2
After mastering the art of formulating high-fire
glazes, Chinese potters were especially noted for
brilliantly colored, glossy surfaces. Today, potters
use similar high-fire glazes (Color Plate 19). Red
copper glaze, China. K'ang-hsi period, A.D.
1662–1722. *© V & A Picture Library.*

Plate 3
Early Islamic mosques were decorated with intricate tile mosaics, glazed in tones of blue and deep purple-black. Due to rules against figures in religious buildings, stylized quotations from the Koran were popular motifs. Tiles in the Karatay Medrese Museum, a former Talmudic law school, Konya, Turkey. Seljuk period, C. A.D. 1251.

Plate 4
Italian Renaissance potters were influenced by Hispano-Moresque ware imported from Spain, producing highly decorated, low-fired, tin-glazed *maiolica* ware. Display plate, from the ceramic town of Deruta. C. A.D. 1530. Diam. 8 in. (20.6 cm).
© Indiana University Art Museum. Photo: Michael Cavanaugh, Kevin Montague.

Plate 5
Red Spiral, a luster-decorated bowl by Judy Trim. Trim burnishes her coil-built bowls with colored slips before bisque firing. She then scratches the design through the slip, and paints on layers of precious metal lusters. These are fired in multiple firings in reduction, building up a rich surface that may take months to achieve. Diameter 15 in. (38 cm). *Courtesy the artist.*

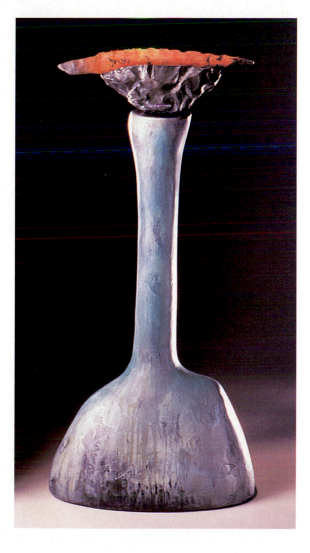

Plate 6
Pedestal Bowl with Weapon Artifact #16, by Richard Hirsch. Hirsch has worked for a number of years with low-fired slips and glaze, layering them and raku-firing them to develop an ancient-looking patina on his enigmatic ritual objects. Now he has added post-firing acrylic lacquer to his ceramic palette. $116 \times 21\frac{1}{2} \times 9$ in. ($15 \times 55 \times 23$ cm). *Courtesy the artist.*

Plate 7

Coiled sculptures in a garden. Juliet Thorne, England, developed a precise coil-building technique to give her figurative pieces their rhythmic structure and surface. (See 3-25 to 3-31 for information on the torso on the left). Hts. 18 and 20 in. (46 and 51 cm). *Courtesy the artist.*

Plate 8

Detail of Mark Messenger's *Ready Made* wall piece (See 4-30). The earthenware slab was carved, modeled, and impressed, then cut into tiles and bisque fired. The final surface on the tiles was achieved with underglazes and glazes, fired twice. The full wall piece measures 3 ft. × 28 in. × 1–2 in (.91 m × 71 cm × 2.5–5 cm). *Courtesy the artist.*

Plate 9

Jardow and Sytheen Together, by Gary Molitor, displays his mastery of multipart mold-making. Cast in porcelain slip, the piece was bisque-fired, airbrushed with matt glazes, then refired. Ht. 13 1/2 in. (35 cm). *Courtesy the artist and the Pence Gallery.*

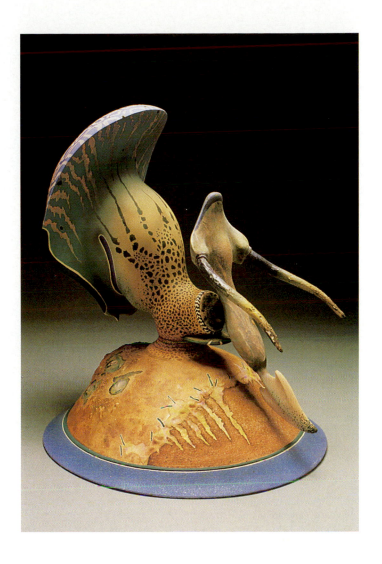

Plate 10

Red Lotus Bowl, by Ross Spangler. The graceful contours and thin walls of Spangler's porcelain bowls display his glowing copper-red glazes to perfection. (See also 7-57 to 7-65.) Diam. 8 in. (20 cm). Ht. 4 in. (10 cm). *Courtesy the artist.*

Plate 11
First Harvest, by Juan Granados. Granados draws on his rich Mexican heritage and his experience as the child of migrant farmworkers, using clay as a medium to access and transform his memories. To create the individual pieces, he builds forms of wadded paper, then lays the clay over them—a process similar to building a piñata. Earthenware, grog, stains, and oxides. Oxidation firing. 12 in. × 8 ft. × 14 ft. (30 cm × 2.43 m × 4.26 m). *Courtesy the artist. Photo: Jon Q. Thompson.*

Plate 12
Charles Spacey, who lives and works in Wales, builds his plates over molds—*wooden molds,* he says, *or anything else that might give an interesting shape.* Influenced by painters Frank Stella and Bridget Riley, Roman mosaics, and American quilts, Spacey uses masking tape, wax resist, and matt glazes to develop his decoration. Then, his carefully worked out patterning is subjected to the atmospheric variations of the kiln, adding an unpremeditated element. Stoneware, ash, feldspar, and clay glazes, colored with oxides and high-temperature stains. 31 × 31 × 4 in. (79 × 79 × 10 cm). *Courtesy the artist.*

Plate 13

Frog Meditates on His Future Endeavors, by Sayoko Kay Mura. Mura used terra sigillata on bisque-fired stoneware to color her meditating frog/bodhisattva/angel. Ht. 29 × 19 × 21 in. (74 × 48 × 53 cm). *Courtesy the artist and the Honolulu Academy of the Arts, gift of Henry B. Clark, Jr., 1994 (7851.1).*

Plate 14

Three tall, fantasy jugs by Edla Griffiths, England. In addition to being decorative, their attenuated forms, beaklike pouring lips, and useless handles force us to think about the kinetics of pouring from a well-designed pitcher. Earthenware. Ht. 16 to 19 in. (41 to 48 cm). *Courtesy the artist and British Crafts Council. Photo: Tony May.*

Plate 15

Soft, cushionlike contours, brilliant color, and richly encrusted decoration distinguish Sara Kotzamani's miniature treasure chests. (See also 3-14 to 3-18.) Stoneware clay, low-fire glazes with a turquoise-glazed "jewel" on the lid. Ht. 5 in. (13 cm). *Courtesy the artist.*

Plate 16

In *The Seduction of Marie Curie,* by Arthur Gonzalez, Curie seems mesmerized by the mysterious gourdlike retorts and pipes. Gonzalez built the torso hollow, pushing out the features from inside. He then developed a rich surface on the figure, using engobes, frit, slips, and glazes, and placed the sculpture against an oil-painted background. Low-fire clay. 26 × 34 × 12 in. (66 × 86 × 30 cm). *Courtesy the artist. Photo: John White.*

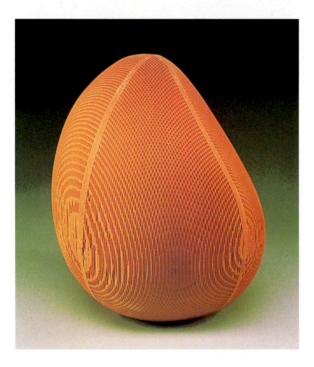

Plate 17

Mango, by Greg Roberts is built of carved honeycomb ceramics (used in filters). Greg has photographed pollens in his backyard, used light microscopy to capture their images, and then rendered them in three-dimensional sculptures as part of a two-year project, *Pollen-nation,* in partnership with the University of California, Berkeley, California. 12 × 12 × 12 in. (30 × 30 × 30 cm). *Courtesy the artist. Private collection.*

Plate 18

Glide Surfshop, Kamakura, by Chris Unterseher. Incorporating hand-built and mold-formed elements in this miniature sculptured scene, Unterseher says it is *a combination of memories from industrial buildings, traditional garden elements, and a real surfshop I saw in Japan.* He stockpiles plaster molds to produce architectural forms and textures. The detail shows him pouring slip onto a mold to make the "corrugated iron" roof of this piece. Stoneware. Length 20 in. (51 cm). *Courtesy the artist.*

Plate 19

Two porcelain vases by Caroline Whyman, England. Her strong, simple, thrown porcelain forms carry complex abstract surface patterns, often based on grids. Her intricate decoration method utilizes carving, inlaid slips and glaze, and sometimes gold and platinum luster in a third firing. Hts. 8 × 9 in. (21 × 23 cm). *Courtesy the artist.*

a

b

Plate 20

Nautical Fountain, by Jessica Abbott, in the Healing Garden at the San Diego Children's Hospital. (**a**) The fountain was built by forming slab tiles over plastic foam replicas of the concrete forms. The handcrafted glazed tiles were then attached with mortar on site. The hollow globe was also built over a form. (**b**) *Seahorse,* fountain detail. Clay, glaze, concrete. 7 × 20 × 2 ft. (2.13 × 6.09 × .60 m).*Courtesy the artist. © Jessica Abbott. Delaney & Cochran, Landscape Architects.*

Plate 21
Sebastian Hushbeck's stoneware vase was fired in double reduction. First bisque fired to cone 05, he then fired it in reduction with a copper base glaze. The final raku firing produced the soft, muted colors. Medium grogged clay. Ht. 16 in. (41 cm).
Courtesy the atist. Photo: Guy Nicol.

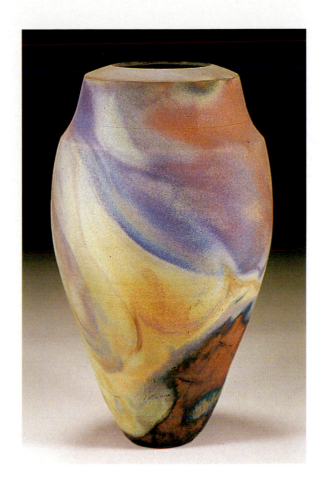

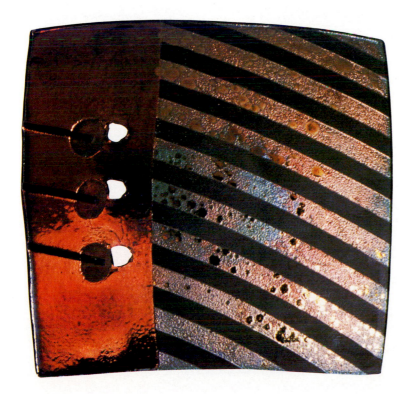

Plate 22
Skip Esquierdo's plates are formed over plaster hump molds. Impressed designs, masking-tape resist, and brushed and spattered glazes create surfaces that echo Esquierdo's background as a print-maker. *I'll try almost anything,* he says, *when looking for new finishes—glue, paint, enamel felt pens, you name it and I've tried it in Raku.* 17 × 17 in. (43 × 43 cm). Raku, reduced in pine needles. Cooled, then placed in cold water to prevent color changes.
Courtesy the artist. Photo: Lee Fatheree.

Plate 23

The vessels in Donna Bruhl's *Spinnaker Series,* like sailboats on different tacks, display varying forms depending on which direction they face. The stripes were achieved with masking tape acting as a resist, over which Bruhl airbrushed color. White earthenware clay, engobes, stains, underglazes, and commercial glazes. *Courtesy the artist. Photo: Donna Bruhl.*

Plate 24

Sadashi Inuzuka, Canada, floats his *Spirit Boats* on a sea of dried slip surrounded by a border of river-washed stones. Earthenware clay. Installation diameter, 30 ft. (9 m). Boats, each 5 ft. (1.5 m) long. *Courtesy the artist. Photo: Peer van der Kruis, courtesy of the European Ceramic Work Centre, The Netherlands.*

Plate 25

Cellular Synchronicity, by Aurore Chabot. Section of a mural for the Marley Building of the College of Agriculture, University of Arizona, Tucson. Hand-made tiles based on organic forms found in nature are inlayed with fossil-like shapes made of the body clay. 12.5 × 8 ft. × 1 in. (3.8 × 2.4 m × 2.5 cm). *Courtesy the artist.*

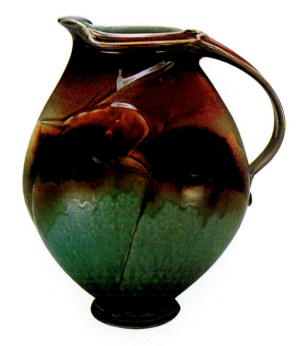

Plate 26

Melon Pitcher, by Steven Hill. Influenced by the swelling shapes of fruits and the colors of swamp vegetation, Hill's multiple glazed surfaces create a fluid, organic glaze application that emphasizes the flowing forms. Single-fired stoneware in reduction, slips and multiple glazes. 11 × 7 in. (28 × 18 cm). *Courtesy the artist. Photo: Al Surratt.*

Plate 27
Regis Brodie's thrown bottle forms are richly decorated using slips, underglaze chalks, underglazes, wax resist, and more slips in carefully controlled layerings. Some of his methods require careful protection from toxic metal salts. Porcelain. Ht. 26 in. (66 cm). *Courtesy the artist. Photo: Regis Brodie.*

Plate 28
Wall Bowls, by Jamie Walker. Walker extended his interest in the tradition of the ceramic bowl as a container/vessel by hanging a group of bowls to be viewed as painting or sculpture. Thrown and handbuilt porcelain with slips and glazes. Oxidation, cone 6.
Courtesy the artist. Photo: Eduardo Calderón.

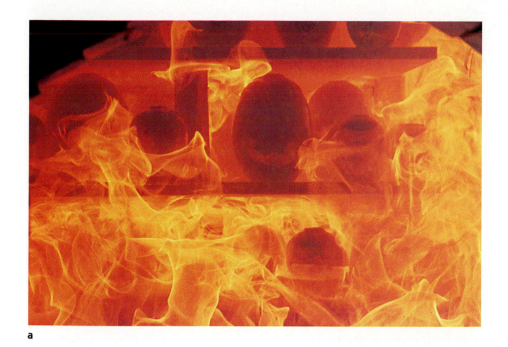

a

Plates 29a, b

(**a**) The interior of Ben Owen's two-chamber wood kiln during firing. The color of a kiln interior is a clue to the temperature inside. Starting out dark and cold, it changes as the heat builds, transforming the clay and the glaze. The color inside the kiln progresses from orange and red tones to yellow to white at the highest temperatures. In a salt-glaze firing the salt is added to the back chamber when the kiln reaches 2350°F (1288°C). (**b**) The front of Owen's two-chamber kiln with Owen raking out coals. *Courtesy the artist. Photo: Kelly Culpepper.*

b

Plate 30

Memory, by Richard Carter, is a twelve-panel wall piece that captures the essence of the human spirit. Carter utilizes elements of the figure and text, which add to the emotional qualities of the piece. He carefully places chemicals that interact with the wood ash during firing, creating unique surface colors and texture on his sculptural works. His understanding of the path of the wood ash and how and where it falls on his work is part of the firing aesthetic. Carter says, *I am interested in pushing the limits of the traditional wood-fired process through the use of various chemical additives.* 48 × 60 in. (122 × 152 cm). Stoneware, found objects, silica rock, oxides. Fired to cone 12. *Photo: Stefan Kirkeby.*

6-8 A bisque mold is useful for pressing clay tiles or making small objects. To make a bisque press mold, Michael Allen rolled out a 1 in. (25 mm) clay slab and pressed a series of face images into the soft slab with a small ceramic doll head. After the slab was left to dry overnight, Allen then perforated the back of the slab with a series of needle-point drying and firing holes every ½ in. (13 mm) and about ¾ in. (19 mm) deep. The tile was fired to cone 05. *Courtesy the artist.*

PRESS MOLDS

You may find it worthwhile to experiment first with press molds of various types—from commercially available plaster molds that will accurately and consistently reproduce your original as multiple casts, to fired clay bisque molds (6-8) that are good for reproducing simple objects, to one-part molds that you can make from clay originals with no undercutting. In addition, any found object, such as a bowl, into which you can press the clay will act as a mold. Whatever the shape or surface of the bowl or object you use for a press mold, its contours and surface will be reproduced in your cast (6-8 to 6-16).

One advantage of a press mold over other types of molds is that it will support the clay so that you can work on the interior surface while the clay is damp, carving or stamping it or even adding modeled or cast forms to create a low-relief sculpture in the interior.

Any carved or **low-relief** decorations on the original will be transferred to the mold. For example, if the original had raised decoration, the mold would show it in negative, and if the original was carved, the mold would show the decoration in positive. The final cast would reproduce the shape and surface of the carved decoration on the original.

6-9 A greenware tile pressed from a bisque mold. *Courtesy Michael Allen.*

6-10 A plaster press mold by Rosanne Reynolds. Reynolds first modeled a clay tile of a raven. She then cast a sturdy thick-walled plaster mold capable of taking the pounding of the clay in the mold.

6-11   After the mold was dry, Reynolds pressed clay into the mold, reproducing a replica of her original raven. After the tile was removed from the mold, she modeled a branch and added texture to the tile. *Courtesy the artist. Photo: Michael Allen.*

6-12   The back side of the raven tile demonstrates how a rib system adds structural strength and helps to reduce warpage. Carving out extra clay reduces the weight of the tile and lessens cracking.

6-13   Peter Chow presses clay into a plaster mold formed from an original tile. He used the one-part press mold to make a series of tiles, then incised drawings on them.

6-14   One way to ensure that the clay is thoroughly pressed against the walls of the mold is to pound it with a rock or other rounded object.

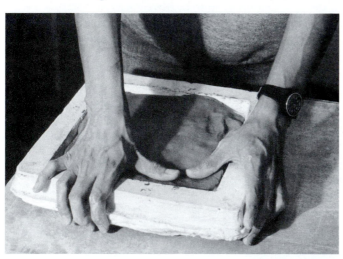

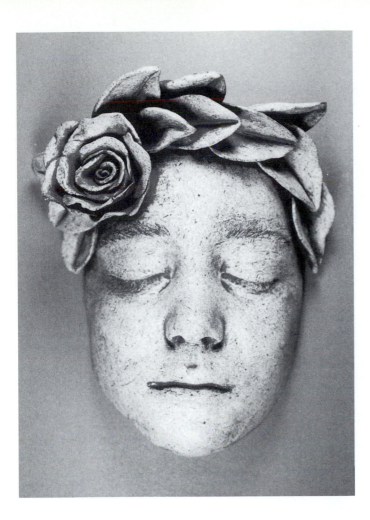

6-15 Pressed molded mask by Sharalyn Lawrence. After the ½ in. (13 mm) thick clay slab was pressed into the mold, it was left to dry until it was damp leather-hard. After it was removed, handmodeled leaves and rose were scored with a needle tool and attached to the forehead with slip. Iron oxide wash, reduction fired to cone 5. *Courtesy the artist. Photo: Michael Allen.*

6-16 Plaster bandage mold of a child. Made from two layers of 1 in. (25 mm) wide plaster bandage strips. The thin mold was reinforced with an additional 1 in. layer of plaster.

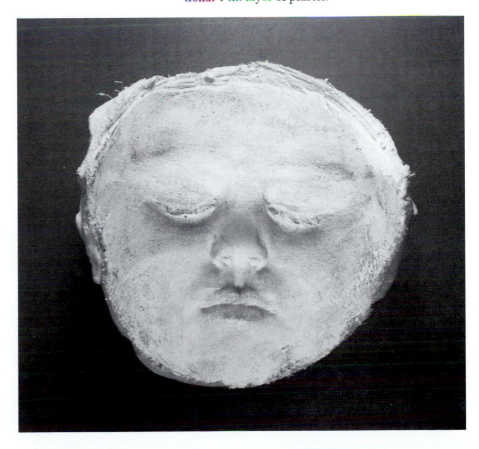

6-17 a Drape molds can be ready-made plastic ones as shown, or you can make a functional drape mold by attaching any flexible material to a frame. **b** Three feet are attached to the bottom of the mold-formed, leather-hard platter after it has been scored and painted with slip.

 TIPS

Fabric, or plastic sheeting nailed to a wooden frame, can make a structurally sound drape mold.

A plaster drape mold will release the clay easily.

DRAPE MOLDS

A drape mold is any support that will hold a draped clay slab while it stiffens to shape. It could be a sling made of cloth or sheet plastic, a depression in a pillow, or a scooped-out hollow in damp sand in a box, covered with plastic sheeting. A drape mold has basically the same purpose as a press mold. But instead of forming the cast by pressing clay into the mold in lumps, lay slabs carefully into the drape mold, patting them in gently rather than pressing them to ensure that the clay conforms to the shape of the mold (6-17). In this case, it is the weight and plasticity of the clay itself rather than the force of your hands that makes the clay reproduce the shape and surface of the mold.

Slabs can also be draped in plaster molds or formed in a drape mold (sometimes called a slump mold) made of flexible material, such as fabric or plastic (6-18), that will allow the clay to settle into soft, irregular forms. Rough-woven fabric will transfer its texture to the slab, while tightly stretched plastic will give the slab a smooth surface.

6-18   Pam Stefl formed the gentle curve of the plate by suspending a slab of clay on a thin plastic sheet and draping it into a plastic container. After the clay became leather-hard, three balls of clay were attached to the back side for feet. Bisque fired to cone 05 (1915°F/1046°C and glaze fired with matt glazes to cone 5 (2185°F/1196°C). *Courtesy the artist.*

6-19   Tiffany Manchip first made a relief sculpture in moist clay. The absence of undercuts allowed her to make a one-piece plaster mold from the original model. This mold was ideal for casting with slip because the slip would fill all the detailing on the face, and preserve it in the final cast.

6-20   After sealing the bottom of a hinged wooden frame with clay, Manchip carefully pours plaster into the frame. Such a frame can easily be removed after the plaster hardens, but you can also make walls from any stiff material or even build them with clay. Manchip mixes her plaster in a ratio of 1½ to 2 parts plaster to 1 part water.

SLIP CASTING

In this process you will be making casts with slip—a fluid mixture of clay and water. Tiffany Manchip made slip casts of her image because the mold allowed her to make several casts that reproduced every facial detail from her original (6-19 to 6-25).

At first, it is best to use a ready-mixed commercial or school slip instead of trying to mix your own. Slip for casting is formulated with a **deflocculant** material, which keeps the clay particles in suspension and the mixture fluid.

Generally, a plaster mold is best suited for slip casting, because the absorbent plaster will quickly draw out the water from the liquid clay, and as the moisture is absorbed, clay walls form against the sides of the mold. When these walls reach the desired thickness, the excess slip is poured out. As more water is drawn from the clay, the walls shrink slightly and pull away from the mold so the cast can be removed easily.

If you learn how to make two-part and multipart molds, you can reproduce almost any form in either a press or slip-casting process (6-26), giving you multiples to which you can add details by carving, incising, texturing, or **sprigging** or glazing.

6-21   A moist clay wall seals the bottom to prevent the liquid plaster from leaking out. The completed mold is left to set.

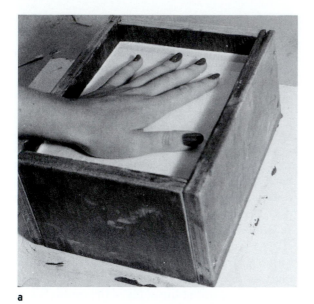

a

b

6-22 **a** To judge if the plaster has set, Manchip places her hand on top of the mold, testing the heat given off by the plaster. Heat is generated from an *exothermic* reaction (a chemical change in which there is a liberation of heat). The plaster is set when it becomes hot. **b** The opened sides reveal the completed plaster mold. Molds can be made using any stiff material—a plastic or cardboard box or even clay for the walls. **c** She digs out the clay from the mold, then carefully washes out any clay clinging to the details. **d** She pours the slip carefully into the dry mold.

c

TIPS

Don't touch the inside of a plaster mold with your fingers. Oil or grease from your hands will stop the plaster from absorbing the slip.

Be sure your slip mold is dry enough to absorb the necessary amount of water from the slip. Slip in a too-dry mold will dry too quickly, so if needed, moisten the mold for a few seconds in water.

Check the mold often to see if the walls are forming.

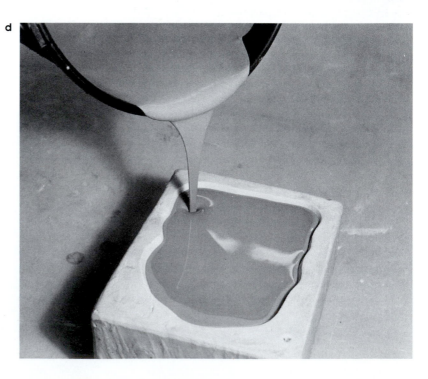

d

6-23 Once the walls have formed to about 5/16 inch (8 mm) thick, Manchip pours the excess slip out into a bucket.

6-24 She then props the mold on two sticks placed across the bucket so that the remaining wet clay will drain from the mold.

 TIPS

Let the cast stay in the mold until the clay has pulled away from the mold and has stiffened enough to allow you to remove it without damaging it.

If, after draining the slip, the cast still looks wet, it is not ready to remove. Wait until the cast is damp dry to the touch before trying to remove it.

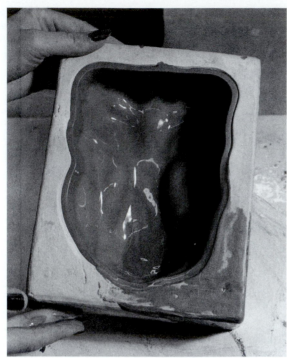

a

 TIP

To speed drying, gently blow compressed air onto the clay, and blow air between the clay and the mold to help release the clay cast.

6-25 a The excess clay has drained out, and the cast remains but is still too wet to remove from the mold. **b** Finally, the cast can be removed from the mold, and the original image is reproduced in detail with walls ¼ in. (6 mm) thick.

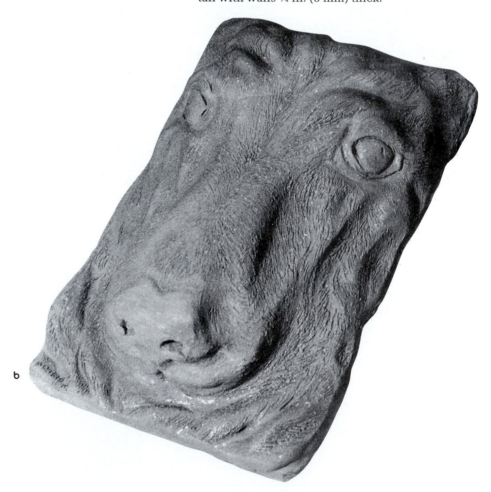

b

MULTIPART MOLDS

Gary Molitor (6-26) has been casting porcelain slip sculptures for many years, using a complex, time-consuming technique to create his mystical, mythical pieces. Starting with careful drawings based on shapes he sees around him—*Often the shapes I start with are biological: microscopic, skeletal, or horticultural*—he builds an original model larger than the final piece, to allow for shrinkage. Then, he makes a multipart mold of each section, and when the model is removed from the original, he pours porcelain slip into it. Molitor says he always makes extra parts, because many are lost in the bisque firing. Next, he applies custom formulated flat glazes with an air brush as well as a clear overglaze. The pieces are fired to cone 6, assembled after firing with epoxy, and mounted on a pedestal inside specially built plastic cases that enhance the appearance of a precious object (Color Plate 10).

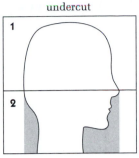

6-27 This original model (left) can be cast in one mold since there are no projections to keep the plaster mold from pulling off in one piece. This original (right) would require at least a two-part mold to pull off successfully.

6-26 *Lau (Longwalk) Tau,* by Gary Molitor. Molitor's cast sculptures are the result of a long process of mold-making, casting in multipart molds, carving, painting, glazing, and overglazing. The results are pieces that appear to be exactly replicated natural objects, but none of these animals/vegetables/birds could be found in nature. Molitor makes many careful drawings based on shapes and objects he sees, but the final results are totally new, mysteriously alive creations. Slip-cast porcelain. Multi-fired to cone 6 (2232°F/1222°C), with a final clear glaze coat. 12 × 19 × 12 in. (30 × 48 × 30 cm). *Courtesy the Pence Gallery, Davis, California.*

KEY TERMS

press mold	plaster mold
bisque mold	undercutting
hump mold	low relief
drape mold	deflocculant
slip-casting mold	sprigging

CREATIVE EXERCISES

1. Make a moist clay slab tile about 6 × 6 in. (15 × 15 cm) and about ½ in. (1.25 cm) thick. Imprint the tile with anything living— your hand, a friend's hand, your pet's paw, a leaf, or the bark of a tree. Make a plaster mold from the original, then replicate it four or five times using the mold as a press or a slip mold. Fire and glaze the tile and insert it into a tiled wall, or hang it in a place that is significant to you.

2. Model a lucky charm of about 4 to 8 inches (11 to 20 cm) to be given to five special friends. Be sure the original does not have any undercutting. Make a mold from it, then slip-cast five copies. If the charm is designed to be worn, punch a hole in the clay before it dries. Remember that the hole will shrink as the clay dries and is fired, so make it large enough for a cord to fit after shrinkage.

NOTES/SKETCHES

CHAPTER 7

The Wheel

If you watch a professional potter throw on the wheel, you will see an almost magical transformation occur in a matter of minutes. The potter takes a lump of moist clay and, in a few apparently effortless movements, transforms it into a cup, a bowl, or a vase (7-7, 7-67; Color Plates 11, 27). Then, with a few more quick hand movements, using a sharp-pointed tool, the potter shapes the rim, then perhaps incises a few lines in the clay to give the piece a personal touch (7-42). Referring to her passion for making pottery, Sandy Simon (9-21) says,

I have had the opportunity to be creative. I am challenged by making a better cup: comfortable, sensuous, contemplative, interesting and different. . . . What I do is important and in some sense is a worship of life itself.

HISTORY: FROM TURNTABLE TO WHEEL

A spinning potter's wheel can be hypnotic. Pottery wheels, however, did not always spin so rapidly or so easily. It took thousands of years of gradual improvement before pottery-forming wheels developed into the compact, variable-speed ones seen in a ceramics studio (1-5). The transition to the wheels we see today began when early potters, using ancient handbuilding techniques like pinching or coiling, found that in order to shape their pots into consistently even forms they needed to turn the pots frequently. The various turning devices they experimented with allowed some potters to become so skilled in handbuilding beautiful vessels (1-2) that they never needed more than a woven basket or fired *puki* (3-20) in which to rotate their work. When, however,

7-1 Early kick wheels were basically the same as those used today. Here, one man opens a bowl, another smooths the interior of a vase. Cipriano Piccolpasso, *The Three Books of the Potter's Art,* Italy, c. 1556. *© V & A Picture Library.*

7-2 Otto Heino in the workshop where he and his late wife, Vivika, made useful and beautiful pottery, also sharing their ceramic knowledge with other ceramists. *Courtesy the artist.*

7-3 By the time the famous Greek potter Exekias was forming and painting this elegant vase around 500 B.C., early turntables had become potter's wheels. 540–530 B.C. *Courtesy the Vatican Museum.*

a more urban way of life demanded a greater output of pots, potters developed more efficient turntables to enable them to make more pots faster with greater consistency of wall thickness and form. The foot-powered **kick wheel** evolved slowly from such early experiments (7-1).

A "true" **potter's wheel** is one that can spin fast enough to produce the **centrifugal force** needed to "throw" a pot (7-2).

Once potters learned to throw on a wheel, they could make utilitarian ware such as dishes, cups, bowls and pitchers, and storage jars more rapidly than before, so older, slower methods were abandoned (7-3, 7-4). For example, long before the Europeans came to the Americas, many advanced ceramic-making cultures on both the northern and southern continents had already been producing complex and beautiful pottery without the wheel. Then potters trained in European techniques came to the New World and introduced new methods. By the mid-seventeenth century, most potters followed the traditions they had brought from their homelands. In the southern United States, where African potters were brought as slaves, their native handbuilding traditions were sometimes combined with wheel techniques to create expressive jars (7-5).

The emigrating English and European potters also found local stoneware clay in the New World from which they made a wide variety of utilitarian ware. Eventually, many of these workshops became semi-industrialized, and much of the work of the potter became mechanized. Despite industrialization, the making of hand-thrown ware in small workshops continued in some places into the twentieth century, and now many potters have returned to the production of hand-thrown utilitarian ware using semi-industrial workshop methods. Other potters have been influenced by the handbuilding traditions of Africa and the indigenous cultures of the Americas (3-20, 6-2). On occasion potters also combine handbuilt forms with wheel forms (7-76).

7-4 The surface of a wheel-thrown pot from the Han dynasty in China shows the rings made on the clay wall while throwing, along with incised decoration generated on a wheel by drawing with a **needle tool** as the wheel turned. *Courtesy of the Royal Ontario Museum, Toronto, Canada, © ROM, Acc. # 918.21.589.*

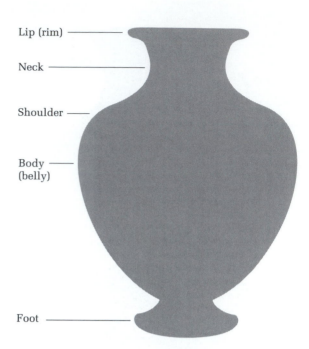

Lip (rim) ————

Neck ————

Shoulder ——

Body ——
(belly)

Foot ————————

7-6   A pot labeled with the terms generally used to describe its parts.

7-5   A thrown and altered *Face Vessel,* attributed to African American potters working in South Carolina in the mid-nineteenth century. The large production potteries relied on slave labor to make utilitarian ware, but it is not known why the potters made these small jugs with their powerful faces. Possibly they had burial significance or religious meaning, or perhaps they were a response to the harsh conditions of slavery. Later, Southern white potters made face vessels for tourist sales. Stoneware, alkaline glaze, with kaolin inserts. Edgefield District of South Carolina, mid-nineteenth century. *Courtesy Division of Social History, National Museum of American History, Smithsonian Institution. (Neg # 55878)*

LEARNING TO THROW

Throwing is the action of making pots on a quickly rotating wheel. The forming of the open **cylinder** that eventually becomes the pot is a matter of control and consistent pressure: It is the pressure of your hands against the soft clay, acting with the centrifugal force of the spinning wheel, that makes the clay rise on the wheel and creates the proper parts and proportions (7-6). The plastic clay, caught between those two forces, has nowhere to go but up.

Learning to throw a series of identical pots, while giving them a personal, creative touch, takes mental and physical discipline. The mastery of the potter's wheel comes from years of training and experience in throwing (7-7, Color Plate 11). For most of us, however, our immediate goal is to throw a passable mug, bowl, or vase, decorate it, and fire it. When you begin to work on the wheel, the type of clay you choose will affect your throwing. For example, a coarse stoneware clay body is more elastic and forgiving than a smooth-grained porcelain body, which will get off center if your movements are jerky.

7-7 This wheel-thrown stoneware pot by Otto and Vivika Heino illustrates the importance of fitting glazes to form in pottery. *Courtesy the artist.*

7-8 Some of the tools you will find useful in the process of throwing and trimming on the wheel. Top: Sponge, two ribbon trimming tools, needle tool, large trim tool (pear pitter). Bottom: rubber, metal, and wood ribs; wire for cutting off the wheel; diagonal wooden trimming tool.

Throwing a lump of clay on the wheel requires using a number of skills and tools (7-8) while simultaneously judging the speed of the wheel in relation to your hand movements. If the wheel speed is too slow and the wall is pulled up too quickly, the result will be an uneven form, or if too much water is added, the clay may wobble out of shape and can spin out of control. If you add too much water to the clay, the wall will become saturated and weak and may flop. If that happens, either use fresh clay or let the clay dry a bit and rewedge it.

Types of Wheels

Be aware that the type of wheel you use can make a difference to your throwing. If possible, pick one that feels comfortable; being comfortable with the wheel will give you more control in the throwing process. For instance, if you have a bad back, a stand-up treadle wheel may be the best choice. On the other hand, you may prefer a sit-down electric wheel. Most commercial electric wheels have enough power for the beginner and have variable speed controls. If you want a wheel that moves in tune with your body, choose a foot-powered kick wheel.

7-9 Jeff Johnson at the potter's wheel centering a 2-pound (908-gram) ball of clay. To start centering he uses one hand, supported and steadied by the other hand.

CENTERING

As Jeff Johnson demonstrates **centering** (7-9 to 7-14), he stresses the importance of using your entire body when throwing. Using what he calls "body physics," he first finds a comfortable position at the wheel, then steadies his forearms against his thighs, legs, or torso and interlocks his hands, thumbs, and fingers. These bracing techniques help him control the clay as he centers. One centering technique he recommends for beginners is to place a stick down the center of a ball of clay, then start to center the ball, watching to see if the stick rotates steadily or if it wobbles. Wobbling means the clay is off center. Johnson says, *Get a visualization of the rod going through the clay. That's your focal point for centering.* After you have compressed the clay ball into a dome, you can then **cone up** the mass. The pyramidal shape of the cone is stable, giving you greater control and manageability in centering the clay. At this point, you can easily see if the clay is either on or off center. If it wobbles, recenter it.

When you begin to work on the wheel, you must learn to understand the various speeds associated with throwing. In the beginning you will center, requiring a medium-fast to fast speed; opening and pulling up require medium speeds; and finishing a piece requires a medium-slow to slow speed.

 TIP

Keep your elbows pressed against your torso for additional support and steadiness during the throwing process.

7-10 Both hands are interlocked at the thumbs to provide additional stability during the initial centering. His left hand applies pressure against the side as the right hand begins to force the clay into a dome.

7-11 With both hands **collaring** the outside of the clay, Johnson completes the first step in centering the lump of clay.

7-12 While using both hands, he methodically applies pressure and squeezes the clay. In the same motion he lifts his hands upward, coning up the clay. This gives greater control and makes centering easier. Some potters cone up twice.

 TIP

Remember to lubricate
the clay with water when
centering.

 TIP

Avoid jerky hand movements
when centering. The slower
the wheel turns, the slower
your hands should move,
and the faster you move the
faster the wheel must turn.

7-13 A centered cone. At this point Johnson will bring the clay back down into a dome.

7-14 A centered dome of clay ready for opening the well.

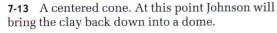

OPENING

Opening (7-15 to 7-20) the **well** in the centered clay establishes the interior base (7-18) of the pot and also determines the pot's diameter and floor thickness. You should leave enough clay at the base so that if a pot is cut off the wheel head, or **bat,** or when the piece is going to be trimmed (7-68 to 7-74), there will be enough clay for a solid base. It is also important to leave enough clay to pull up.

The opening process is done in two steps. First, center your index finger over the clay and make the initial hole. Then, widen the opening while pulling your hands and thumbs outward. This creates a well in the clay.

 TIPS

Stick a pin tool into the base of the clay to check the thickness of the base.

Don't make a base too thin. If you do, you will slice through the bottom of the pot when you cut the pot off with a wire.

7-15   With his right hand gently pressing against the wall, Johnson pushes in his left index finger at a slight angle, to start the well, pushing until its depth is about ⅜ to ½ in. (10 to 13 mm).

 TIP

Keep your forearms firm when opening the well.

When making the well, while pushing down into the clay, you can gain additional stability by resting your thumb and index fingers against each other.

7-16   Using both hands to collar the clay on the outside, Johnson presses his thumbs into the well, curling them outward as the wheel spins. This completes the well.

7-17   Cutaway view of the well showing the hand and thumb position. The base of the well is ½ in. (13 mm) thick, leaving enough clay for trimming a foot (7-68).

7-18 Johnson establishes the floor of the well. His left hand is angled downward, fingers slightly curled. With the wheel spinning at about medium speed, he guides his pulling hand toward his body with his right hand.

7-19 Cutaway view of the well showing the hand positions.

a   b   c

7-20 Cutaway view of **a** centered ball of clay with opening, **b** the well widened, **c** centered well ready for pulling up the wall.

 TIPS

Before widening the well, add a little water for lubrication.

Rest your hands on each other when opening the well to provide stability.

7-21 To pull up the wall, Johnson lubricates the clay with water and gets the wheel going at slow to medium speed. He braces both hands together, locking his thumbs or resting one hand on the other. Do what is most comfortable for you.

PULLING UP THE WALL

When you are **pulling up** the wall (7-21 to 7-26), the speed of the wheel should be medium. Pulling up usually requires two to three pulls to make the wall rise and to attain an even thickness. Start pulling up, all in one motion, squeezing the clay with your fingers while slowly lifting your hands up. The speed at which you pull up will be affected by the wheel speed: The faster the wheel spins, the faster you can pull up. In the beginning, it is best to start slowly until you have gained control over the process.

After pulling up the wall, trim off any extra clay left at the base with a wooden diagonal tool. As a final step in finishing a cylinder, trim the **lip** (or **rim,**) with a pin tool (also called a needle tool) to even it (7-27a); then use a chamois, sponge, or plastic sheeting on the top to smooth the lip. Remove the cylinder by pulling a wire tool (7-27b) toward you between the cylinder and the wheel head.

 TIPS

Move at an even pace—not too fast—when you squeeze the clay and pull up the walls. Too-fast movement may make one part of the wall too thin and another too thick.

When pulling up the wall, keep your hands touching each other for added stability and control.

Remember to add a little water before pulling up the cylinder.

 TIP

When making the first pull on the wall, brace your hands and arms so that they are steady. Pull up the clay slowly.

7-22 Johnson pulls up the wall a second time. He squeezes the clay between his index and middle fingers while lifting his hands upward.

7-23 He evens out the lip. In one motion, his left finger and thumb squeeze the clay, while his right index finger levels off the edge of the lip.

7-24 Johnson trims and finishes the base of the cylinder with a wooden diagonal tool.

7-25 Johnson pulls up the wall a third time, slowing the wheel speed as the cylinder begins to take shape.

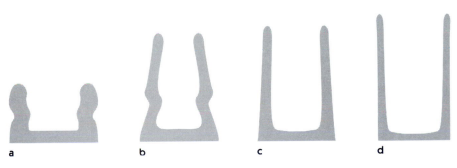

a   b   c   d

7-26 Cutaway drawings show making the cylinder: **a** base established, starting to pull up the walls; **b** extra clay pulled up; **c** cylinder walls established; **d** completed cylinder with thinned walls.

7-27 a Johnson levels off an uneven lip. With the wheel at a slow speed, he gently slices into the rim with a pin or needle tool. He carefully lifts off the excess. Next, he will cut the cylinder off the bat with a wire (see drawing). **b** To separate the vase from the bat, you can use a cutting wire or thin nylon cord. Stop the wheel head and place the cutting wire flat on the bat. Hold one side of the wire down with your thumb. With the other hand, and with your thumb pressing down on the wire, pull it toward your body.

a

b

7-28 After pulling up the wall, Mary Law defines the lip and evens it out by pressing the clay between the second and third fingers of her left hand, while the sponge in her right hand presses down on the edge of the rim.

THROWING A MUG

Throwing a mug is a logical continuation from a cylinder (7-28 to 7-33) and will also give you a chance to think about the aesthetics of a container (7-40). Consider such aspects as its weight, the rim (or lip) thickness, and spiraling ridges, called throwing rings. The shape of a pot, no matter how simple, can be pleasing to the eye. A mug can also evoke emotions through its tactile quality, as we think of holding a warm mug of tea or coffee or sharing a moment with family or friends.

Mary Law makes cups and mugs that range in form from large, flaring to small, elegant forms. Demonstrating opening and pulling up a mug she says, *I open with my right hand over my left, then I pull back to widen it in the same way. I always widen it a little bit more than I want the piece to be. Then I collar back in.* From that point on, it is a matter of pulling up the wall, **ribbing** the outside and setting the rim of her mug, then preparing to pull and attach a handle.

 TIPS

Straighten out the outside wall of the cylinder with a rib. Push gently from inside against the rib.

The more pronounced the throwing rings you leave on a pot, the greater the color contrast will be in a transparent or semi-opaque glaze.

7-29 Mary Law pulls up the wall, using the left-hand middle fingers in a slightly curled position on the inside of the cylinder. Her right-hand index, first, and second fingers on the outside press into the cylinder wall.

7-30 The clay wall begins to rise. Both of her hands apply equal pressure inward, while she pulls upward as the clay revolves on the wheel head.

7-31 **a** Ribbing the outside of the cylinder to complete the wall. **b** A wood rib is used to straighten the wall of the cup. The rib is held at about a 135-degree angle as the wheel head spins counterclockwise. The left hand and fingers gently push the clay into the rib.

7-33 Mary Law with a completed mug ready to be lifted off the wheel and placed on a ware board to dry.

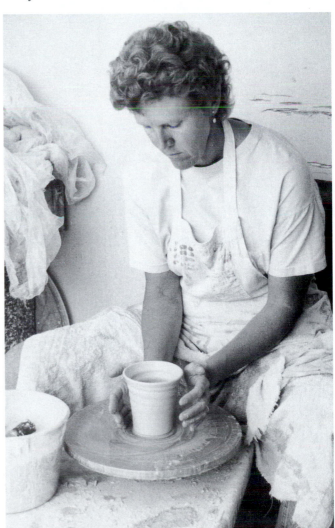

7-32 A sponge tool is a sponge secured to the end of a wood or metal handle. It is used to absorb excess water from the well of a pot and is especially useful in narrow and deep cylinder or vase shapes, too difficult to reach by hand.

 TIP

Sponge out excess water from the well before removing the mug from the wheel. This helps avoid cracking in the bottom of the mug.

TIP

Attach handles when the mugs are at a soft leather-hard state, but still flexible.

7-34 Mary Law pulls a slug of clay into a long, tapered cone, in preparation for making handles for a series of mugs.

7-35 After cutting the slug into short strips, she applies slip to the point where the handle will be applied at the top of the mug. The mugs are at a soft leather-hard stage but still have slight movement, or flexibility.

7-36 Law attaches the handle to the slipped area, pressing to make a good join.

7-37 She turns the mug horizontally so that the handle dangles vertically, free for pulling.

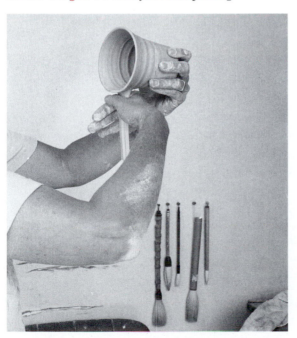

PULLING A HANDLE

Pulling a handle and attaching it to your mug not only involves learning a technique, but also calls for aesthetic decisions about the size and shape of the handle in relation to the mug. Handles not only should be pleasing—echoing or contrasting effectively with the shape of the mug—but there is also utility to take into consideration: A handle should be easy to hold and should support the weight of a full mug in your fingers. In addition, the space between the handle and the mug should be large enough so that your knuckles do not touch the burning hot side of the mug.

Mary Law usually pulls handles for mugs or cups in groups of seven or eight at a time, dividing the process into two stages. She calls the first stage the "wet" stage, which includes pulling and attaching the wet handles to the mugs (7-34 to 7-40). The second step is the "dry" stage in which she clips off the extra length of clay, then presses the handles to make flanges in the clay. This widens them at the point of attachment to the mug, strengthening the join (7-36).

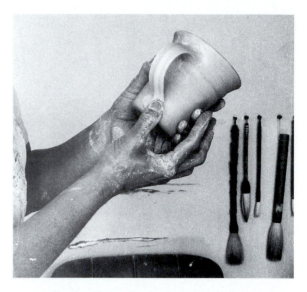

7-39   After applying slip to the mug, Mary Law presses her thumb into the lower end of the handle, bonding it to the cup. She says, *I kind of rock it. I go around it. I'm really pressing the clay onto the pot.*

7-38   Pulling a handle requires a small amount of water to lubricate the clay and numerous pulls to establish the length and shape. Mary Law says, *I keep turning the cup around. I use my thumb to form ridges in the handle.*

7-40   A group of mugs, thrown by Mary Law. Stoneware. *Courtesy the artist. Photo: Richard Sargent.*

THROWN FORMS

Potters find sources of inspiration in the forms of rocks, animals, flowers, machinery, mountains, buildings, or boats. When you think about the forms you could use in your ceramics, you may consider geometric shapes such as the cubes of buildings or the pyramids of rooftops, fluid forms like water or a jellyfish, organic forms like gnarled trees, or geologic features in the landscape such as rocks and mountains (7-41 to 7-43).

The forms of the human body are also important as sources of inspiration to potters. This is seen in the many figurative vessels made throughout history (8-4).

Some of the terms that apply to pottery are based on the human figure. When you studied the form of a labeled vase (7-6), you saw how the ceramic terms that described its shoulder, foot, lip, neck, and body were linked to the human body. Other forms created by ceramists are based more abstractly on the scale, weight, shape, and proportions or texture of the human body.

7-41 Steve Branfman's elegant bottle was made with a combination of coiled and thrown parts. Its form is strong enough to carry the bold, abstract poured and brushed glazes. Ht. 28 in. (71 cm). *Courtesy the artist.*

7-42 *Melon Pitcher,* by Steven Hill. Hill draws most of his inspiration for his organic forms from southern cypress swamps. His glazes also are based on the rich textures and mossy tones of cypress swamps. (See also Color Plate 26.) *Courtesy the artist. Photo: Al Surratt.*

7-43 Janet Mansfield, Australia, takes a classic urn form that goes back to the early days of pottery and gives it contemporary freshness with her free line decoration and modern interpretation of ancient wood firing techniques. *Courtesy the artist. Photo: Roger Deckker.*

7-44 Tim Frederich finishes the vase by using a wooden diagonal tool to remove extra clay and shape the base.

THROWING A VASE

As you go through the steps in throwing a vase (7-44 to 7-56), Tim Frederich says, *Take your time, and go slow when pulling up the cylinder wall.* It is important to throw the cylinder thick enough, because as the wall is raised and the clay is pushed out with a rib to form the curve, it will become thinner and thinner as the clay is stretched. If the clay is stretched too thin or too much water is used as a lubricant, the form may collapse.

After you have thrown the cylinder and the body has been pushed out to form a slight bulge, the next step is to **collar in** the shoulder. Lubricate the wall with a sponge and place your hands around the upper section of the cylinder in a choking position. As the wheel spins, push in and move your hands upward. Next, use a rib to shape the outside and around the rim. Finally, refine the lip with a chamois, piece of newspaper, or thin plastic sheeting. You can use a sponge attached to the end of a long stick (called a sponge tool; see 7-32) to absorb excess water in the bottom of the vase.

7-45 With the wheel spinning at fast speed, Frederich centers a 3½ lb (1.59 kg) ball of clay. After centering, he makes the well by pushing his left hand and fingers down the middle of the clay dome. Frederich then leaves ¼ to ⅜ inch (7 to 10 mm) of clay on the bottom. He pulls his fingers toward his right hand to widen the well, while curling his right hand around the outer wall for stability. This helps maintain a "true" outer wall.

7-46 With the wheel spinning at medium speed Frederich raises the wall of the centered dome. The middle fingers of both his hands are pressed together slightly while he makes the first pull.

7-47   After each successive pull on the cylinder, he levels the rim and compresses it by gently squeezing the clay between the index finger and thumb of his left hand. He holds his index finger on the right hand horizontally, lightly touching the rim. As it turns, pack the upper edge of the clay while leveling it.

 TIPS

Throw your cylinder thick enough to provide enough clay to allow you to stretch out the wall of the vase.

Remove excess water with a sponge from inside the vase before collaring in the neck.

 TIP

Throw the vase on a bat instead of directly on the wheel head to avoid distorting the vase when you remove it.

 TIP

Drizzle a little water on the rim before leveling it.

7-49   Narrowing the neck is called collaring in. This is done with the wheel spinning at slow speed. Hold both your hands apart so that your index finger and thumb are facing each other and are in a horizontal position. Gently squeeze the clay in-and-up in one motion, narrowing it with each successive collaring in.

7-48   The second pull is made all in one motion starting at the bottom of the cylinder. Frederich gently presses into the wall of the clay while slowly pulling up with his two middle fingers on both hands.

7-50 Frederich shapes the outer and inner wall of the cylinder with wooden ribs. The left hand presses against the inside wall with a rib, while the right hand ribs the outer wall.

7-51 He uses a wooden rib to add decorative lines to the rim.

7-53 Tim Frederich with a finished vase. Frederich says, *A well-thrown pot should have even wall-thickness throughout.*

7-52 With the wheel spinning at slow speed, Frederich drapes a damp chamois over the edge to finish the rim of the vase. He holds it in place over the rim between his index finger and thumb of his left hand, while his right hand carefully pulls the end of the chamois around the rim, rounding the edge.

7-54 A stoneware vase with a blue green glaze by Tim Frederich. Fired in an oxidation atmosphere to cone 5½. Ht. 8½ in. (22 cm). *Courtesy the artist. Photo: Tom Siegel.*

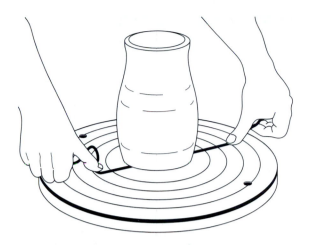

7-55 After Frederich trims the base with a diagonal tool (7-44), he cuts the piece off with a cutting wire. With the wheel in the off position, Frederich holds the cutting wire between his thumbs and index fingers of both hands. With his thumbs pushing the wire against the wheel head, he holds one side still, while he pulls the other side of the wire toward his body keeping it taut and as flat as possible as he makes the cut. He leaves the vase on the bat and removes both from the wheel head.

 TIP

When pulling the wire through the base of a piece, slowly turn the wheel head. Beginners may want to stop the wheel head completely when cutting a piece off the wheel.

7-56 Cutaway drawings show how a basic cylinder is transformed into a vase: **a** the cylinder after one pull; **b** the cylinder after two pulls; **c** the cylinder after three pulls, and the neck collared in at the shoulder; **d** the completed vase with the curve of the belly shaped from the inside using a wooden rib. A chamois is used to round the edge of the rim.

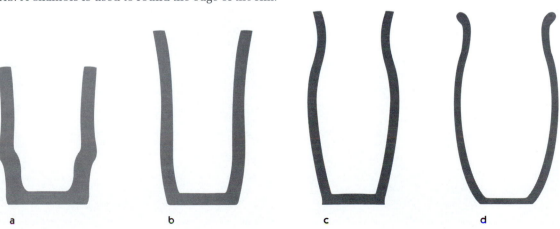

a   b   c   d

THROWING A BOWL

Throwing a bowl (7-57 to 7-67) can be a satisfying experience that calls on all the skills you have learned so far, as well as some new ones. As when you throw any shape, use some method of anchoring your arms. Ross Spangler demonstrates throwing a thin-walled, elegantly curved bowl. Spangler says, *When centering, what I do is anchor my elbow into my hip and use my body as the force. I use my opposing fingers and push with my hands and my hip.*

When you widen the well and begin to pull up the wall of the bowl, you must be aware of the profile of the curve. The clay you use should be pliant enough to shape easily, but not too wet; otherwise, the wall may be unable to support the weight of the clay as the bowl flares, and the bowl might slump.

7-57 Opening the well. Ross Spangler pulls the clay with his fingers toward his body.

 TIP

Use the fingers on one hand to push down into the wall to refine the curve when giving shape to a bowl.

 TIP

To shape a bowl, move your fingers down and toward the center. Keep the pressure even and the wheel speed constant but not too fast.

7-58 Spangler presses the clay wall out to begin shaping the bottom of the bowl. In forming an elliptical profile, he says, *I feel it is important to make a gradual curve when forming the bottom.*

7-59 Spangler collars in the wall. This brings the clay wall into a thicker piece, which is necessary to provide enough clay for pulling up the wall of the bowl.

7-60   Spangler pulls up the wall. On his first pull, he pinches the clay with his thumb and first finger raising the collar of the clay to an even thickness, which brings the height up to 5 in. (12.7 cm).

7-61   Spangler completes the second pull, refining the cylinder as he begins to flare out the wall while he continues to thin the wall to get ready for the third and final pull.

a   b   c

7-62   Cutaway drawings show **a** opening the well of a bowl; **b** widened well, wall pulled out and up; **c** completed bowl.

7-63   Spangler pulls the wall up and outward at the same time, establishing the final wall thickness.

TIP

To avoid deforming the rim, gently release your fingers outward when you reach the top of the bowl.

7-64 Spangler finishes off the rim of the completed bowl using a piece of plastic sheeting or chamois.

7-65 Spangler often uses a mirror to help him see the shape and profile of a bowl while throwing.

7-66 Some wheel forms developed from cylinders.
Row a: Small cylinder: **1.** Wide rimmed cup.
2. Vase with concave profile. **3.** Bottle shape.
Row b: Tall cylinder: **1.** Tall vase. **2.** Narrow necked, bulbous bottle. **3.** Bottle with wide shoulder.
Row c: Small wide cylinder: **1.** Tea bowl. **2.** Salad bowl. **3.** Soup bowl.
Row d: Wide cylinder: **1.** Flat-based bowl. **2.** Wide bowl. **3.** Wide rimmed bowl on narrow base.

TIP

To check on the developing shape and profile of your work as you pull up the wall, prop a mirror in front of your wheel.

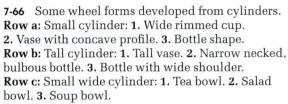

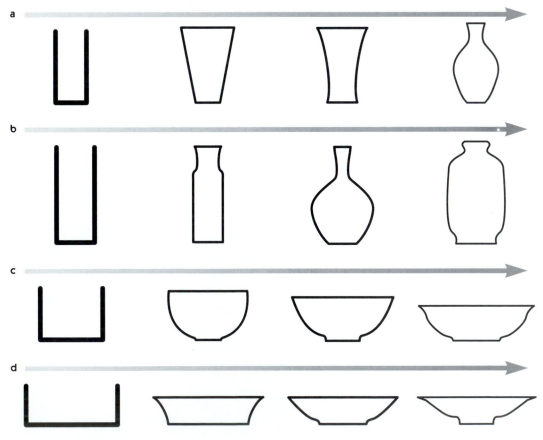

Wheel Form Chart

PROFILE Ross Spangler

Ross Spangler, writing about his years as a potter, says,

I was lucky. I got my start in ceramics when I was eleven years old. Clay is a fantastic thing to get exposed to at a young age. Even luckier, my father Glenn was a teacher and a potter. He was a proficient thrower, methodical with glazing and systematic about firing the kiln. I soaked up his teaching with great enthusiasm and wonder. What I loved most about my dad's art was his ability to pour refinement into each piece he threw. I held his vision of a cleanly executed form as my ideal, a model of clay working that has stayed with me ever since.

As a teenager I began using porcelain exclusively—completely. First, it's the most difficult clay to master on the wheel. Second, porcelain glaze formulas can be fairly complex. Also, firing the kiln to produce the colors correctly required a lot of practice. With my father's guidance, a drive to learn, and growing passion for using clay as an art form, I grew into a potter. With time and ex-

7-66 Spangler holds the completed bowl. After allowing it to dry to a leather-hard state, he will trim it in preparation for glazing.

perimentation I evolved into a full-time potter. By twenty-one I had a collection of production work that I would sell regularly to wholesale clients. My aim was to be a successful potter. Going to college for an art degree wasn't a priority. Working with my father in his studio was more important.

From the beginning I always created my pottery in a style that was akin to the Chinese and Japanese aesthetics. Over 900 years old, porcelain pottery from the ancient Ch'ing and Sung dynasties retains a delicateness and refinement in potting that was/is a high watermark in human history. Porcelain was only one of many achievements of Chinese potters.

My experience in throwing porcelain inspired me to strive for the same beauty and artistic excellence as these early Chinese and Japanese wares.

For me as a ceramic artist, glazes and form become the key to creating great pots. And consistently getting good results from my clay, my wheel, and the kiln has become a lifelong passion. Other types of ceramics from raku and ancient Greek vases to contemporary sculpture all influence my work, but the early years of learning the classic form and color of the Chinese helped forge an important foundation for my future direction as a contemporary potter. (Color Plate 11).

7-67 Ross Spangler's vase forms are sure and elegant. The rutile and black iron decoration over a white glaze on this one emphasizes its upward spiral as if it is growing naturally on the wheel. Stoneware, fired to cone 10. Ht. 10 in. (25 cm).

TRIMMING

Trimming (7-68 to 7-74) is the term for shaving or paring off excess clay at the base and shoulder of a piece of pottery. Trimming is most easily accomplished when the clay is leather hard, which means the clay is damp, but not so soft that it slumps when handled. Trimming reduces the weight of the pot and refines its shape. A well-trimmed foot gives a bowl a sense of lightness. A trimmed foot also serves several purposes. It will raise the pot off the table surface, giving it a more elegant look, and also provides a hand hold when you are glazing the pot.

Some potters throw as thin as possible to eliminate trimming and make a foot by simply tapping the bottom of a pot with the palm of the hand. This dents the base into a concave shape, which helps prevent the pot from rocking on a flat surface. A pleasantly proportioned bowl can be further enhanced by trimming the outside curve to match the inside curve.

7-68 Bill Cravis trims the foot of a leather-hard bowl.

7-69 An assortment of ribbon tools used for trimming ware in the leather-hard state: **1** general tool (pear pitter) for flat, broad areas; **2** square end and round tool for medium-size work; **3** curved end tool for trimming the foot and body; **4** large square end tool for trimming flat, broad areas; **5** square and round end tool for small work.

 TIPS

As soon as a pot is firm enough to move it without distorting the shape, invert it, then let the base dry to leather-hard before trimming.

If you plan to dip the pot when glazing, trim the foot high enough so that you can grip it with one hand.

7-70 Cravis first trims the shoulder of the bowl to determine the contour and to establish the width of the foot. His decision is based on aesthetics and a desire for stability of the fired bowl.

7-71 After establishing the diameter of the foot, Cravis marks the width of the foot at ³⁄₁₆ in. (5 mm). Beginning at the center and closely following the interior contour of the bowl, he trims out the foot ⁵⁄₁₆ in. (8 mm) deep, leaving the center slightly lower than the edge.

 TIP

Bevel or round the edge of the foot slightly to keep sharp fired edges from scratching tables or other surfaces.

7-72 Cutaway drawings show trimming a bowl: **a** inverted leather-hard bowl, ready to trim; **b** shoulder trimmed, with the base diameter established; **c** center of the base trimmed out, the foot completed.

7-73 Concentration is an important aspect of working on the wheel. Rachael Sande has learned it well as she trims a bowl on a kick wheel at Kevin Nierman's Kids 'N' Clay ceramics studio. *Courtesy the artist and Kevin Nierman.*

Trimming with a Chuck

Some potters, like Lauren Lui, prefer to use a hollow bisque-fired ceramic tube called a **chuck** (7-74) for trimming. It has a flared top that holds a vase or bottle in place, resting on the shoulder of the pot. This protects narrow-neck vase shapes, or precarious pieces with delicate lips that might get damaged or tip over if placed directly on a wheel head for trimming.

7-74 **a** Lauren Lui inserting a vase into a bisque-fired ceramic chuck. First the chuck is centered on the wheel head, and then attached to the base with three pieces of soft clay. *Courtesy the artist. Photos: Michael Allen.*

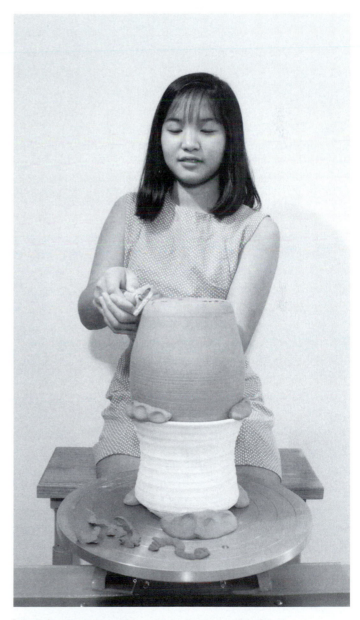

b Lui demonstrates trimming a vase in a chuck using a ribbon trim tool. After the damp clay vase is set into the chuck, it is secured with three clay coils.

7-75 A porcelain soup tureen by Carol Temkin was made to hold 48 ounces (1.4 liters) with a matching ladle. A delicately shaded combination of turquoise glazes was used. *Courtesy the artist. Photo: Robert Arruda.*

7-76 One of a series of *Communicating Vessels* by Jules de Balincourt and Jim Piercey. In many cultures, clay vessels were used as symbols of the soul of the departed, so it is perhaps not surprising that de Balincourt and Piercey should turn wheel-thrown forms into heads. Ht. 15 in. (38 cm). *Courtesy the artists. Photo: Aaron Sturtz.*

ALTERED FORMS

You can extend the possibilities of the wheel by altering (7-75 to 7-77) the shape of your work while it is on the wheel or after it has been removed. Just pinching the lip of a thrown cylinder will finish the form and make it pour properly. But the possibilities go much beyond such changes made for functional reasons. For example, you can throw a pot and squeeze in the sides to make it oval or paddle it until it is squarish. You can cut pots apart, rearrange the parts, then join the parts together again to make a totally new composition. Thinking about how you can alter and recompose your wheel-thrown shapes can help you develop a fresh aesthetic approach to working on the wheel.

You can also use the wheel as a tool for forming shapes that you will later combine with slabs or coils to create forms for sculpture.

7-77 *Cypress Pitcher,* by Steven Hill. This large
wheel-thrown and altered stoneware pitcher was
inspired by the stump of an old cypress tree in
a swamp and decorated with multiple sprayed
glazes. Ht. 21 in. (53 cm). (See Color Plate 26.)
Courtesy the artist. Photo: Al Surratt.

KEY TERMS

kick wheel	well
potter's wheel	bat
centrifugal force	pulling up
needle tool	lip (or rim)
throwing	ribbing
cylinder	pulling a handle
centering	collaring in
cone up	trimming
collaring	chuck
opening	

CREATIVE EXERCISES

1. Throw a set of mugs specifically designed for a picnic basket. Glaze them with your favorite colors or designs that reflect how you feel, and then go to the park for a picnic and use the mugs.
2. Make a flower vase to decorate a table for a holiday gathering. Throw two or three cylinders, alter them, and rearrange the parts into a container. Select fresh or dried flowers to fill the vase.
3. Throw a set of bowls that will be used for a special dinner party or event, and invite some of your friends to enjoy your pottery.

NOTES/SKETCHES

CHAPTER 8

Surfaces

So far, you have worked with a number of processes for forming damp, plastic, leather-hard, or liquid clay, becoming aware of the many ways there are to transform this earthy material with your hands and tools. You have seen how clay can be formed into useful, interesting, beautiful, or expressive objects with these methods. Now, in this chapter, the illustrations show some of the different methods that creative potters and sculptors use to change the surface or color of their work. From the earth colors of the Mayan jars (Color Plate 1) to the brilliant copper red glazed porcelain from China (Color Plate 2), to the maiolica-decorated plates of Renaissance Italy (Color Plate 4), over the centuries potters have developed numerous ways to embellish their ware. Today, there are even more decorative techniques available to the ceramist (Color Plates 5, 6, 13, 14, 19).

By studying the surface treatments shown throughout the book, you will better understand why so many artists use ceramics as their decorative or expressive medium and why the dedicated ceramist never tires of experimenting. For example, Steven Hill was inspired by the rich color and smooth surfaces of the muddy, slow-flowing water and vegeta-tion of a swamp to create a series of pitchers on which the deeply colored glaze decoration swirls and flows (Color Plate 27). Other artists, like Patrick Siler (8-25), use slips on green-ware plates to depict scenes that, despite their contemporary imagery, recall how early Italian potters painted mythological scenes on platters for merchants to display. Ron Nagle decorates cups that show the influence of Japanese tea bowls but were not designed for drinking (8-48). Nagle layers multiple glazes and sprays china paints on the fired clay in a personal interpretation of a decorating material that for hundreds of years was associated with flower-painted teacups. Potters Otto and Vivika Heino (8-34) and Maija Grotell (8-39) always related the texture, color, and tactile quality of their glazes to their thrown forms. Sculptors Arthur Gonzalez (8-22 to 8-24, Color Plate 17) and Frans Duckers (8-28, 8-47) emphasize the form and enhance the expressive quality of their work through the sensitive use of oxides and slips. Sayoko Kay Mura uses terra sigillata on bisque-fired stoneware to bring color to her sculpture (Color Plate 14). Carol Molly Prier, on the other hand, places her pots in a pit fire and lets the fire imbue them with color.

HISTORY

For thousands of years, humans have in some manner transferred religious symbols, joyous stories, evidence of status, visual puns, domestic decorations, intimate personal messages, and hundreds of other visual and tactile experiences to the surface of moist clay or fired ceramic objects.

For many decades, archeologists considered that the discovery of the ceramic process in an early culture indicated that the group had left their nomadic, hunting/gathering lifestyle to settle as village-based farmers and that the need for domestic utensils for storage and cooking was the only motivation for developing ceramics in early societies. Recent excavations, however, have revealed that in some areas groups of fishers, hunters, and seasonal nomads also initiated ceramics technology. Although often the need for domestic utensils does appear to have been the main motivation for developing ceramics, some archeologists now suggest that the initial impetus was sometimes due to the desire of high-ranking members of a group to display their superior status or their religious beliefs. In that case, the clay provided an easily available surface on which to imprint, carve, or paint a message.

Whatever aesthetic, religious, status-seeking, or creative urges led to the embellishment of ceramic surfaces, there is little doubt that throughout history the surface has been as important to potters and sculptors as the form, even when enhancing the surface was not necessary to an object's function. For example, the potter making a large *pithos,* on Crete over two thousand years ago, had no functional reason to create designs with his thumb on the reinforcements at the coil joins (3-4, 8-1), but the storage jars that still stand in the ruined storerooms of Minoan palaces show great ingenuity in the range of thumb designs impressed on their utilitarian surfaces. To be functional, the early pot from Japan did not need the row of decoration the potter (8-2) gave it; nevertheless, the pot would lack individuality without the decoration. Ladi Kwali's incised decoration on a water jar was not essential to its function, but it adds visual emphasis and character to the swelling body and neck of the pot (8-3). The potter in Peru who portrayed an individual so vividly on a stirrup pot and used the burnished surface of the clay as a painting ground was as concerned with surface as with

8-1   The urge to decorate seems to be a universal human trait—perhaps it is a way of identifying oneself in a place or time. Large storage jars like this one made for a Minoan palace on Crete about 1400 B.C. were coil-built in sections. To add structural reinforcement, the Minoan potters placed an extra coil around the vessel where the sections were joined, and they usually created patterns on the applied coils by pressing their thumbs into the moist clay. *Photo: James McGann.*

8-2   Even the earliest potters decorated their pots. This pot, dating from between 10,000 and 12,000 years ago, came from a cave in Japan. Its textured decoration was named *Jōmon* by archeologists (the word means straw or rope design), who applied the term to all later periods of similarly decorated Japanese pottery. *Courtesy the Museum of Archeology, Kokugakuin University, Tokyo, Japan.*

8-3 Ladi Kwali, a Nigerian potter, demonstrates decorating, emphasizing the pot's swelling form with vertical lines and the neck with horizontal patterning. *The Field Museum, Chicago (Neg. GN 82515.31).*

8-4 Early ceramic decoration sometimes had ritual, ceremonial, or status significance, and the painted facial decoration on this mold-formed vessel from Peru may indicate the rank of the person whose portrait it depicts. From the Mochica culture, Trujillo, Peru, A.D. 200–600. *Courtesy of the National Museum of the American Indian, Smithsonian Institution (#34205).*

form (8-4). In the American Southwest, the indigenous potters working in the Mimbres culture developed abstract design to a fine art on plates and bowls made for ritual or funereal rather than domestic use (8-5). In the Islamic tradition, the relief patterns and lustrous color on tiled prayer niches had a religious purpose (8-6), displaying quotations from sacred writings, but the religious function of the tiles did not deter the makers from creating beauty on the ceramic surface. The meditative pose of a Buddhist statue from China expresses a spiritual state rather than an individual's appearance (8-7), but the statue's aesthetic impact is also enhanced by the muted three-glaze surface applied over the stoneware clay.

TEXTURE

Imagine running your hand over the satiny surface of a burnished pot (8-14) or the smooth skin of a sculpted face (5-15), then pretend to place your hand on the textured surface of Maija Grotell's pot (8-39), Ben Owen's jug (8-9), or Regis Brodie's vase (8-33). Your varying tactile responses to these pieces demonstrate

8-5 In the indigenous American Mimbres culture, bowls like this one were buried with the deceased. Using the clay surface as a painting ground, the maker of this bowl created a possibly symbolic design whose meaning we cannot interpret but can enjoy as an abstract composition. Mimbres Valley, New Mexico. *Courtesy Arizona State Museum, University of Arizona. Photo: Helga Teiwes.*

8-6 The arch on this press-molded tile from a tomb in thirteenth-century Persia echoes the form of the *mirab,* or prayer niche, in Moslem mosques. The twining floral patterns and inscriptions are typical of Islamic tile decoration, as is its beautifully glazed surface.
© V & A Picture Library.

8-7 This life-size Buddhist *lohan,* sculpted in China during the Liao dynasty (A.D. 907–1125), was placed in a cave with a number of similar statues. Realistically modeled, the figure wears robes colored with the three-color glaze combination characteristic of the earlier Tang dynasty. In a shadowy cave this statue must have been awe-inspiring. From the I-Chou caves.
Copyright British Museum.

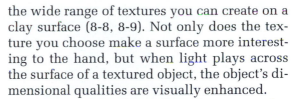

8-8 Soft, damp clay can be decorated by pressing, rolling, stamping, or scratching. Look for likely objects around your home, in the studio, or in a junkyard. You can also carve stamps from plaster, wood, or clay. From top to bottom: pine branch, threaded pipe, carved plaster stamp, metal mesh, fork, rock, pencil, saw-cut wood block, piece of rope.

the wide range of textures you can create on a clay surface (8-8, 8-9). Not only does the texture you choose make a surface more interesting to the hand, but when light plays across the surface of a textured object, the object's dimensional qualities are visually enhanced.

You can texture the surface of a pot or sculpture when it is damp, leather hard, or dry. Damp clay can be scraped smooth, stamped, modeled, or decorated (8-8) using any tool or object you find in your home or studio; for example, a dried corn cob rolled across the impressionable surface or a piece of metal mesh will leave an interesting imprint in damp clay. Even after some drying has occurred, the leather-hard clay can be textured with incised lines, with carved relief, (8-9) or by **sprigging** with appliqué decoration.

Try to pick a textural surface that will increase the work's expressiveness but not overwhelm its form.

8-9 a Ben Owen III, at work at the wheel carving a vase. He is using a chuck to hold the piece in place. **b** A covered jar by Ben Owen III. The carved surface contrasts with the elegantly thrown lidded form. Stoneware clay, salt glaze, with iron slip. 11 × 11 × 22 in. (28 × 28 × 56 cm). *Courtesy the artist.*

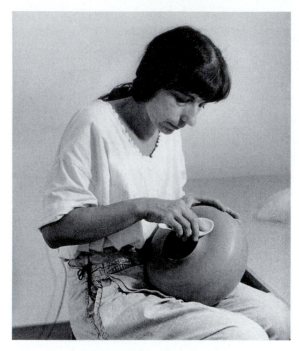

8-10   Inspired by the work of the Hopi potter Nampeyo (1860–1942), Carol Molly Prier burnishes her pots, then pit-fires them, allowing the fire to enhance their color (8-14). Here, she burnishes a pot using the back of a porcelain Chinese soup spoon, saying, *What is wonderfully handy for me is the curve of the spoon. It can fit into a lot of tiny spaces.* Stroking the surface of the pot she sets up a rhythm, working in whichever direction is the most comfortable.

BURNISHING

Burnishing is an age-old method of finishing the clay surface. It was used in the past to make porous low-fired pots more nearly watertight. Burnishing compresses the clay particles and helps to close the pores of the clay, resulting in a smooth, gleaming surface that is more moisture resistant than uncoated clay. Burnishing smooths the clay and imparts a glossy surface to ware. It is widely used today for coloring or embellishing pots or sculpture (8-10 to 8-14, 8-26), often in combination with **terra sigillata** slip, which can bring color to the surface. Judy Trim (Color Plate 5) burnishes, then applies colored slip and layers of metal lusters on her bowls.

Burnishing is accomplished by rubbing the clay surface with an object such as a spoon, a piece of smooth wood, a metal rib, or a stone. Each person develops an individual way of burnishing, tending to favor particular tools. Using a clay body with no grog, or very fine grog, will help keep coarse particles from coming to the surface and causing scratches as you burnish.

Carol Molly Prier burnishes in three stages: first, on the trimmed, damp leather-hard pot; second, when the ware is hard to leather hard. At the second stage she says, *I use a flexible metal rib because it has a very wide surface. I curl it up and hold it and start rubbing.* Finally, when the clay is bone dry, she applies vegetable oil, lets it dry for about ten minutes, then burnishes the surface with a hard object such as a smooth rock.

8-12   Prier sometimes burnishes with the back of a kitchen spoon but finds that even the edge of a metal spoon can't fit in certain curves. She says, *Some people say that if you use a silver spoon some of the silver will come off onto the clay. It does give color—in a pit firing it can give blues or a dark olivey color.*

8-11   Prier burnishes a hard–leather-hard surface with her favorite tool, a flexible stainless steel **rib** that she folds around her index finger. She says, *The reason I use a rib is because it has a wide surface area and doesn't leave little lines in the clay.*

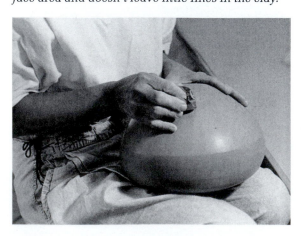

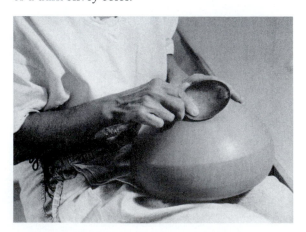

8-13 Once her burnishing is done, Prier **bisque-fires** her pots, then re-fires them in a pit fire (8-14). After firing, she gives them a final finish by polishing them with a carnauba-based wax, rubbing the surface gently with a soft cloth to bring out the lustrous fire-produced colors.

TIP

For additional polish, rub carnauba-based wax on the pot after firing (see Color Plate 14).

8-14 A wheel-thrown, burnished, and pit-fired pot by Carol Molly Prier. Inspired by handbuilt Native American ceramics, Prier works in a personal manner, preferring to throw her pots to attain a smoother surface than is possible with hand-built ones. *I love this shape, she says, because it comes from the traditional shape. But I can only throw a certain size because of the weight of the clay.* Courtesy the artist. Photo: Charles Frizzell.

8-15 Slip made from a smooth white stoneware clay is applied to a leather-hard vase with a soft *hake* brush. To help get an even coat, the vase is rotated on a banding wheel while the slip is applied. *Photo: Michael Allen.*

8-16 Using a squeezable rubber syringe called a slip trailer, you can create a line drawing or design with contrasting slip.

ENGOBE AND SLIP

The terms **engobe** and **slip** are often used interchangeably. Both are mixtures of semiliquid clay and water that provide an opportunity to change the color of your entire pot or sculpture, to add a contrasting color, or to bring tactile and visual interest to your work (8-15 to 8-26). (These engobes and slips are different slip mixtures than those used for slip casting.)

The earliest potters and sculptors did not have glazes with which to decorate their work or to make the surface smooth or watertight, but they found they could use mixtures of clay and water to cover an entire sculpture or decorate areas of a pot in contrasting colors, adding textural and aesthetic interest. Slip could also fill the pores, making the clay somewhat impervious. The slips the early potters used were often made of clays in which certain minerals predominated—such as an iron-rich **terra-cotta** that gave a reddish brown color. Although the colors were limited, the potter who mold-formed the Peruvian portrait vessel (8-4) made effective use of whatever coloring materials were available. When a greater variety of clays with higher firing possibilities became available, slips were formulated with white porcelain or brown stoneware, extending the range of the surface color available. Nowadays, slips and engobes are colored with commercial stains and oxides in greens, blues, yellows, and browns, extending their decorative range. Caroline Whyman carves her porcelain pots and inlays colored slips to achieve textured patterns (Color Plate 20).

As a result, today's clay artist can work in a painterly manner with slips. For example, Agnese Udinotti applies colored slip to a white plate, then, in a subtractive process, rubs away the colored slip until a figure emerges, revealing the white clay undersurface against a dark slip background (8-20). Patrick Siler coats a piece with a thick coat of black slip and sticks stencils cut from blotting paper on the wet black slip. He then covers the entire piece with an ivory-colored slip and lifts the stencils off revealing the figures in black (8-25). Richard Hirsch, on the other hand, uses a very fine slip known as terra sigillata, which he burnishes, then enhances with layers of glazes (8-26), and Arthur Gonzalez uses a combination of oxides and slips on his sculpture (8-22 to 8-24; Color Plate 17).

SGRAFFITO

Sgraffito is a decorative process in which you scratch through a layer of slip to a different colored clay beneath—or to a different color of underglaze on the clay body (8-17, 8-18; Color Plate 5). It is an ancient process. The painters of Greek pottery used it to incise delicate details of clothing and armor through the terra sigillata slip coating on vases and drinking vessels to the clay underneath. In a less intricate manner, European country potters and early potters in colonial America used sgraffito to decorate their jugs and plates, often in combination with **slip trailing**. Drawing through an applied slip or underglaze can be done with a special sgraffito tool, a needle tool, or any sharp instrument such as a nail, a dentistry tool, or a chisel-pointed tool (8-19).

To decorate your work with sgraffito, apply the slip or engobe to a damp or leather-hard piece. Leave it to dry for an hour or two, or until the slip still feels damp but does not smear when handled. This coating of slip, properly applied, will provide you with a surface that can easily be scratched through with a clean line; later, clean off any trimmings left in the line with a soft brush. If you let the slip dry completely before beginning your sgraffito decoration, the line may end up with a slightly ragged edge.

Rebecca Niederlander combines sgraffito with underglazes to reveal her drawings in contrasting color (8-17), and Agnese Udinotti sometimes uses the scratching technique on her slip-coated plates (8-20).

8-19 A sgraffito tool is a chisel-pointed tool used to decorate pottery or sculpture by scratching through a layer of colored slip to the clay body underneath.

8-18 To demonstrate the traditional sgraffito technique, three coats of white clay slip were painted onto a damp, leather-hard vase. The slip was left to dry completely before a curvilinear design was scratched through the surface with a curved metal cleanup tool, exposing the contrasting color of the clay underneath.

8-17 A sgraffito-decorated vessel by Rebecca Niederlander. She first applies two or three coats of low-fire underglaze on the greenware, then when the underglaze is dry, she paints a different color on top of it and scratches through the top layer of the underglaze. Dreamlike figures appear through the second coat in the underglaze color. *Courtesy the artist. Photo: Andrew Gillis.*

TIP

For damp slip or underglaze, use a somewhat blunt-tipped tool; for a drier surface, use a sharper tool.

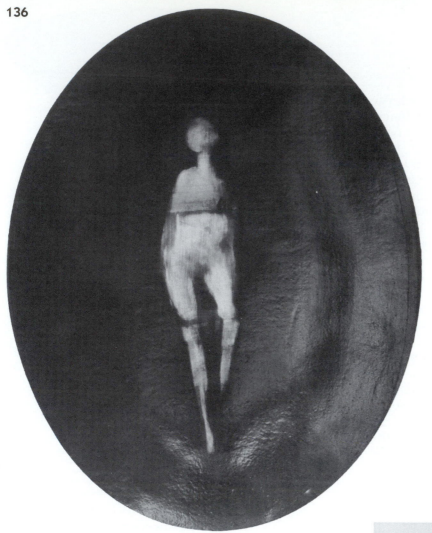

8-20 Agnese Udinotti created this *Shadow Image, 262* plate using subtractive slip techniques. To achieve the effect of a ghostly figure, she first applied a coat of white slip to the greenware, then painted black slip over the white. She then rubbed away the black slip with her fingers or a damp sponge, and scratched through the slip with a knife using a sgraffito technique. *Courtesy the artist.*

TIP

Blend colored underglazes or slips while damp for subtle color transitions.

8-21 A section of a wall piece titled *CDI,* by Jules de Balincourt (4-28). Modeled in relief on slabs, the surface is sharpened with freely incised, carved, and painted detail. Its painterly surface was achieved by the manner in which de Balincourt brushed on the high-fire slips that he applied to the sculpture. *Courtesy the artist. Photo: Cida Fukushima.*

8-22 Arthur Gonzalez applies a coating of dry **frit** (ground-up glassy material) to one of his fired sculptures. He rubs it in well, then sponges and brushes on a variety of colored slips, working them well into the surface. Their subtle color emphasizes the emotional qualities of the piece while accentuating its sculptural forms (see 5-17 to 5-20 for his forming methods).

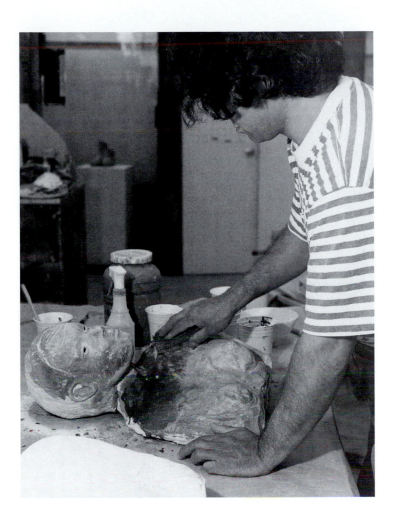

8-23 Gonzalez rubs the frit onto the surface, which helps the colorants stick to the clay during firing. The amount of frit used will affect the quality of the surface. Wear gloves and a respirator when using frit.

8-24 Gonzalez uses a variety of brushes to wash on and blend the colored slip, working it into the frit. His complex, layered technique imbues the surface with a lyrical quality.

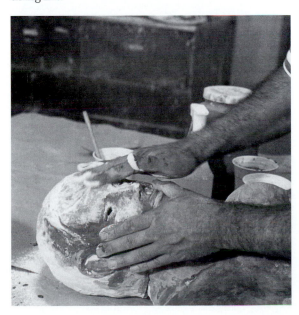

8-25 *Admiring the Results,* by Patrick Siler, depicts a contemporary potter's response to a successful firing, but the scene could have taken place in a potter's shop hundreds of years ago. The image was made with two colors of slip in a resist method, using blotting paper for stencils. Diam. 19 in. (48 cm). *Courtesy the artist. Photo: Arthur Okazaki.*

8-26 *Vessel and Stand #2,* by Richard Hirsch. Hirsch first applies two or three coats of terra sigillata, then airbrushes on more color. He burnishes the surface, glazes it, and raku-fires it, in a layering technique he has developed that creates an ancient-appearing surface. Ht. 8 in. (20 cm). (See also Color Plate 7.) *Courtesy the artist.*

TERRA SIGILLATA

Terra sigillata is a very fine grained, smooth solution of slip used to coat pottery and sculpture. Because the clay used is so fine, it bonds well to the clay body. The terra sigillata should match the type of clay body used; generally, a low-fire clay. Burnishing the applied terra sigillata slip after it dries will give the surface a silky and lustrous sheen (Color Plates 7, 13). The rubbing action during burnishing helps the terra sigillata cohere to the clay body surface (8-26). A low firing temperature will help preserve the burnishing. Here is a recipe you can test to see how it works on greenware tiles (4-27):

RECIPE FOR WHITE TERRA SIGILLATA BASE

Note: The base and colorants can be mixed either by weight or by volume.

VOLUME	WEIGHT	
5 tablespoons Kentucky Ball clay OM4	25.0	gm
⅐ teaspoon Frit 25 or any available frit	0.625	gm
⅕ teaspoon sodium carbonate (to help the slip stay suspended in the water)	1.25	gm
11½ tablespoons water	100.0	gm
COLORANTS: ¹⁄₂₅ teaspoon cobalt (blue)	0.25	gm
⅓ teaspoon iron (brown)	1.20	gm
¹⁄₁₂ teaspoon copper oxide (green)	0.75	gm

Note: Weighing chemicals and water on a gram scale provides the most accurate results.

Choose one of the oxides and add it to the base color. To lighten or darken the color, add less or more oxide. This recipe makes enough to paint about fifteen to twenty 1¾ in. (32 mm) square tiles.

Mix all the base ingredients together. Separate the mixture into batches. To color the slip, add an oxide of your choice: cobalt oxide for blue, iron oxide for brown, or copper oxide for green tones. Then pour the mixture into a straight walled 4 oz (118 mL) clear glass or plastic jar. Let the mixture stand until you see the slip separate and the heavier particles set-tle to the bottom. Carefully pour off the water, reserving the fine top material; discard the coarser residue and repeat the process two or three times until a fine slip remains. The settling process can take one to several days.

If you want to color the slip, add ¹⁄₂₅ teaspoon of each of the three oxides to separate batches of slip and fire them. Repeat with more colorant if the tone is too light. Paint the slip onto the greenware tiles and test-fire them to see if the terra sigillata fits your clay body without peeling or cracking off when it dries and is fired. Fire the tests to cone 012 (1623°F/884°C) to cone 010 (1661°F/905°C).

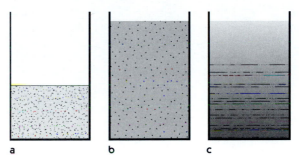

8-27 a Blend the Kentucky Ball clay OM4, frit, and sodium carbonate (soda ash) in a 4 oz (118 mL) straight wall jar. **b** Add 100 fluid grams of water to the powder, place a lid on the jar, and shake it until the mixture is blended. **c** Wait one to three days, or until the heavier clay particles begin to separate from the solution leaving a layer of murky amber-colored water standing at the top. Carefully pour off this water, take a sample from the top layer of slip, and apply it to a test tile. It may be necessary to let the slip settle out longer, pouring off additional water that has separated from the solution.

8-28 Frans Duckers, the Netherlands, paints oxides onto his life-size sculpture *Harrie,* a commission for a bank in Holland. Duckers says he likes to position his sculptures where they will create or enter a dialog with the people present; he says, *The sculpture evokes verbal reaction from the passerby. Courtesy the artist. Photo: Veronique Jean.*

OXIDES AND STAINS

Oxides are natural earth materials that are important components of clay and glazes, but metallic oxides such as cobalt, copper, and iron can also be used for coloring clays and glazes. In this chapter we are dealing with their potential for enhancing the surface of pottery and sculpture (8-28, 8-29, 8-47, 8-49). (For the use of oxides in glazes, see pages 144 to 156.)

The range of possible colors that oxides can provide is extensive. For example, red iron produces terra-cotta reds to brown tones; cobalt yields a wide range of light pastel to dark blues; chromium can produce greens, pinks, or muddy browns; and copper gives greens, light blues, or deep maroon reds.

Stains are coloring materials that include metallic oxides such as cobalt, copper, nickel, and chromium as well as tin, titanium, manganese, zinc, and zirconium. These stains are manufactured to provide the ceramics industry with colors that are consistent in hue from batch to batch. Now they are also used by potters and sculptors for coloring clay bodies and porcelain casting slip, and as surface color washes. In a different approach, Greg Roberts (Color Plate 18) uses special nonfired stains to accentuate the forms of his sculpture.

8-29 Red iron oxide sponged onto a bisque-fired tile provides color on the surface and accentuates the relief. After the excess oxide is sponged off, the tile can be glazed with transparent glaze, then fired.

 TIP

Apply oxides in thin washes to avoid peeling or inducing an overglaze to crawl. Or you can re-bisque the stained tile to "set" the color, then glaze the work.

UNDERGLAZES

Underglazes have been in use at least since Chinese potters painted on cobalt designs with underglaze to provide color on their famous blue and white ware. The great advantage of underglaze colors for a beginner is that, unlike glaze, the colors stay basically the same when fired so that as you paint you can have an idea how your work will look after firing. For the same reason, they are popular with artists who like to work in a painterly manner (8-33, Color Plate 27). Underglaze colors can be applied as washes and as bands of color (8-30), and they are excellent for fine line work such as lettering or painting hard-edged designs (8-31).

Commercially prepared underglazes can be either opaque or translucent, and come in various forms such as crayons (chalks), pencils, watercolors, or pens (8-32). Use them on bisque surfaces in the same way you would use nonceramic painting or drawing materials on paper. There are also underglaze inking pads you can use to stamp on designs.

The freedom that commercial underglazes give the artist make them popular, but there are a few guidelines for their use. For example, some underglazes can be used on greenware and others can be used only on bisque-fired ware. Underglaze colors can be blended or mixed, except for pinks, maroons, and some reds and oranges that are especially susceptible to contamination and do not blend well. If you do try blending those colors, make tests to see how they react when fired.

As the name implies, underglazes are generally used under glazes, with a transparent glaze usually applied over them to bring out the underglaze colors. Used in this way, low fire glazes and underglazes can bring brightly colored decoration to nonfunctional pottery (Color Plate 14).

8-30 Bill Cravis paints a band of translucent blue underglaze onto one of his bisque-fired vases. He prefers to apply banded decoration on a potter's wheel because he can keep it rotating at a steady speed. After bisque-firing the vase, he will apply a transparent glaze and refire it. Cravis says, *I use underglazes because they offer me a wider range of color possibilities than is available with oxides, which tend to be limited to blues, greens, or browns. I am attracted to pastel colors such as pinks, soft beiges, light purples, and oranges.*

8-31 An opaque black underglaze painted onto a bisque tile holds the crisp edge made by the brush. The underglaze will maintain the edge without blurring after a transparent glaze is applied and the tile is fired.

a

DECORATIVE UNDERGLAZE TECHNIQUES

8-32 Underglazes come in various forms for decorating bisque-fired ware. A painterly effect can be achieved by using various methods of underglaze application singly or in combination. **a** Crayons are good for background work or broad designs. **b** Pencils work well for shading or fine line work. **c** Pan watercolors give translucent wash effects. **d** Squeezable pens produce slightly raised lines.

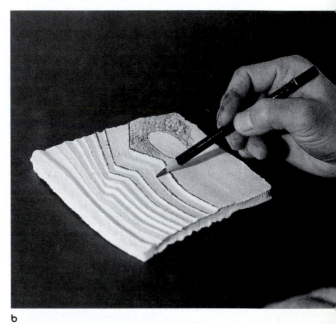

b

c

d

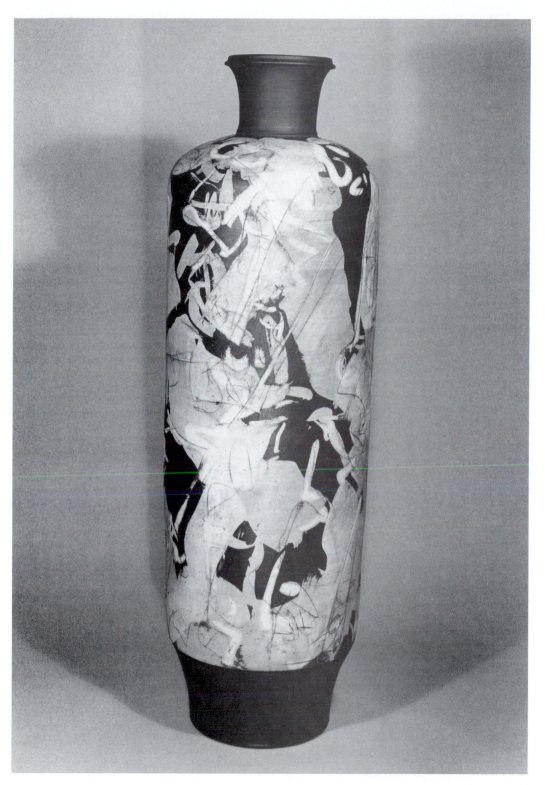

8-33 *Large Form #3,* by Regis Brodie, who makes use of his painting and drawing background and his interest in abstract expressionism and postmodernism to create images on his large vessels. He relates his work to that of the Chinese Sung potters, whose classic style is humane and natural. (See also Color Plate 27.) Slips, underglaze, chalks, glaze. *Courtesy the artist.*

GLAZES

In ceramics, a **glaze** is any glassy coating that has been melted onto the clay surface by the use of heat (8-34 to 8-36). Made up of a solution of minerals and water, a glaze must be subjected to the heat of the kiln for a certain length of time to melt and come to maturity. When it cools it becomes hard and dense and develops its full color. From the beginnings of glaze making in Egypt and Crete, through the early uses of glaze to decorate small sculptures and cover tiles with brilliant color, potters have continued to learn from experiments, or from accidents, creating a wide variety of surface effects with glaze. Two of the main motivations behind early experimentation were to develop a coating that would make the clay impervious to moisture and to cover the dull tones of the clay with glowing color or with a white background to show off decoration.

Assuming that you decide to make a glaze, you should understand the role of the three essential components that make up a glaze, and you will need to learn what happens to the compound when you fire it. The three main glaze components are **fluxes,** such as sodium, potassium, calcium, lithium, and zinc, which help a glaze melt in the heat; a refractory, alumina, which increases its viscosity and stabilizes it; and the principal glass former, silica. These basic components are found in various materials and may be combined with metallic oxides or stains to provide color, surface texture, or mottled effects. They also control whether the glaze will be matt or opaque.

Glazes are generally divided into high-fire glazes, medium-fire glazes, and low-fire glazes. These glazes mature at different temperatures and duration of firing, and within these three categories, glaze types range widely from the brilliantly colored low-fire glazes to matt, to satiny, to gloss, to the medium-fire earth tones. They include high-fire glazes such as porcelain and stoneware glazes; salt glaze, wood ash glaze (Color Plates 5, 6, 22, 28) each of which has a unique, characteristic appearance.

A low-fire glaze (Color Plate 14) is an applied coating that never completely fuses with the clay body, whereas a properly fired high-fire glaze actually fuses with the silica in the clay body and becomes integral to the ware. When this vitreous (glassy) state is reached, the fired ware becomes impervious to water. A properly chosen, applied, and fired glaze can enhance the beauty of form, add definition to wheel-thrown lines, give your work a mirror-like quality, bring contemporary decoration to the surface, or, if it is a **matt glaze,** give your work a satiny surface that can suggest warmth and age.

8-34 This wheel-thrown pot by Otto and Vivika Heino shows the ripple effect of the throwing rings made by the potter's fingers when pulling up the wall. The bold brush strokes create dramatic surface decoration. Vivika Heino once wrote, *The function of beauty is as much of value as the function of service: a small-neck bottle, for example, may be just as enhancing to a room—whether it is empty or holds a branch of blossoms.* Stoneware, high-fire glazes. *Courtesy the artist.*

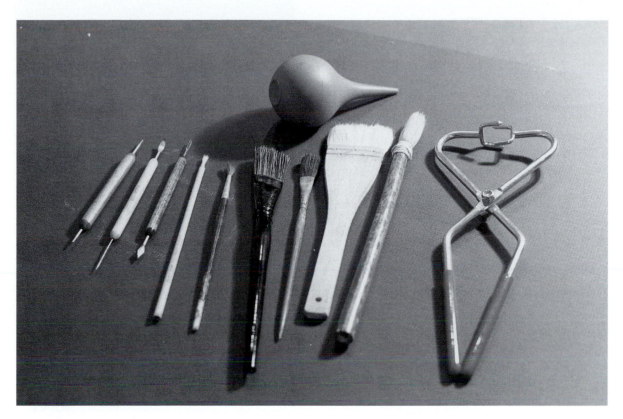

8-35 A variety of tools that can be used for glazing and decorating. Left to right: sgraffito tools; brushes for applying slips, oxides, glazes; tongs. Above: slip or glaze trailer.

8-36 **a** Passing a dipping glaze through a 30-mesh sieve eliminates large particles and hard lumps. **b** A viscous glaze is screened through a 30-mesh sieve using a flexible spatula. For finer screening, use a 50- to 100-mesh.

a

b

MIXING AND TESTING GLAZES

If you go further in ceramics, you will need to learn more about the chemistry of glazes and how the heat of the kiln and its atmospheric conditions affect glaze colors and texture. In the meantime, mixing the measuring spoon recipe given here will start you testing your own glazes. Keep a spirit of adventure as you carry out your tests and try different amounts and combinations of colorants. First, cut some slabs into small tiles, then bisque-fire them before applying the glazes for the tests (8-37).

RECIPE FOR LEADLESS CLEAR GLAZE

Cone 05 (1915°F/1046°C)

VOLUME	WEIGHT
5 tablespoons Frit 3195	35.0 gm
1¾ tablespoons EPK China clay	8.0 gm
½ teaspoon Bentonite	1.0 gm
3½ tablespoons water	29.0 gm

YIELD: 76 fluid grams (79.41 mL)

Blend the dry materials with the water in a cup. Pour mixture into a mortar, and grind with a pestle for two or three minutes, until the mixture is smooth and creamy, without lumps. If you prefer, mix the glaze and sieve it through an 80-mesh sieve.

The recipe yields about 4½ tablespoons of glaze. Divide into three 1-tablespoon batches and mix a different colorant into each in the following amounts:

Blue: add ¹⁄₁₆ teaspoon (1 pinch, or .25 gram) cobalt oxide

Green: add ¹⁄₁₆ teaspoon (1 pinch, or .25 gram) copper oxide

Brown: add ¼ teaspoon (5 pinches, or 1.00 gram) red iron oxide

Fire the tiles at cone 05 (1915°F/1046°C).

 TIP

Before applying glaze to bisque ware, damp sponge your piece, or hold it under running water for less than a second.

8-37 To make and test a basic low-fire glaze, you will need a set of measuring spoons and three small bisque-fired tiles.

 TIP

Rinse off the bisque ware before applying glaze. This helps eliminate dust, minimizes pinholes, helps the glaze flow evenly, and keeps the glaze from drying out too quickly.

APPLYING GLAZE

The manner—the number of coats, dipping, spraying, or brushing—in which you apply a glaze depends on the effect you want to achieve. Although some potters prefer to apply glaze to greenware, usually it is applied to bisque-fired ware, which is stronger and less susceptible to breakage than raw, unfired greenware. It is also important not to handle bisqued ware because the oil from your fingers can keep the glaze from adhering properly—one more reason to wear gloves when working with glaze.

You can brush, dip, pour, or spray a glaze on, depending on the type of glaze or the type of surface you want (8-35 to 8-47). Before glazes are applied, they should be **sieved** to eliminate any lumps, foreign matter, or contaminants (8-36). Sieving will allow a brushed glaze to flow on more smoothly and quickly. Sieving will also refine the glaze chemicals that could clog a spray-gun orifice. Glaze applied with a brush (8-38, 8-39) requires two or three coats, except for transparent glaze, which is best applied in one or two thin coats. After a glaze has been brushed, dipped, or poured on the bisque-fired surface, it will change rapidly from a shiny wet to a dull appearance. At that point you can apply the next coat. For a variety of unique effects, you can blend glazes, apply one color on top of another, or, in the case of glazes painted next to each other, allow them to bleed into each other.

When you are glazing pottery, the application should be about 1/64 in. (1/2 mm) thick. The outside wall of pottery or sculpture is usually glazed to about 1/8 in. (3 mm) from the base or foot to avoid glaze dripping down the piece, causing it to stick to the kiln shelf.

8-39 Maija Grotell, photographed in 1950, applies a glaze with a *sumi* brush to one of her wheel-thrown stoneware vessels. Finnish-born Grotell often carved a piece first, then glazed it with deep-colored glazes, creating rich surfaces that were appropriate to her strong forms. She constantly tried new glaze effects, handing on her excitement about glaze experimentation to students. *Courtesy of Cranbrook Archives. Neg. #CEC940.*

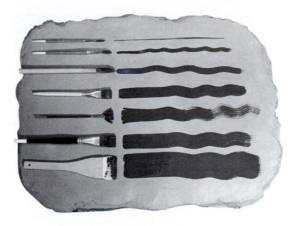

8-38 Brushes for applying underglazes, glazes, slips, stains, or oxides come in a variety of shapes and sizes. Long-bristled *liners* hold plenty of slip, engobe, glaze, or oxide and are good for making lines; blunt-pointed *sumi* brushes are used for painting with stains or oxides or for general glazing; and wide, flat brushes will cover large areas.

8-40   Jeff Johnson applies one coat of liquid wax resist with a soft brush to the bottom of a bisque-fired square dish. The wax prevents the glaze from adhering to the piece when it is submerged in the glaze.

TIP

Diluting the wax resist with 50 percent water will make it easier to apply.

DIPPING A GLAZE

Dipping a bisque-fired piece of pottery or sculpture into a bucket of well-sieved glaze is a tried and true way to coat it with glaze (8-40 to 8-45). Before glazing, coat the base of the ware with either a liquid wax (8-40) or water sealer, to minimize glaze clinging to the base. Wear gloves and use tongs when dipping, and when dipping by hand, hold a piece by as small an area as possible to avoid leaving finger marks. Usually a piece is submerged in glaze for only a few seconds, and the consistency of the glaze, whether you dip it once or twice, and how long you keep the piece in the glaze, will all affect its final appearance. You may prefer to use one coat of thick glaze or two coats of a thinner glaze mixture, based on your own experience. After a piece is glazed, it dries to the touch relatively quickly, usually within a few minutes. After you lift the piece from the glaze, give it a quick shake and turn the piece to ensure that excess glaze is drained from the interior and exterior. Small glaze drips beaded up and clinging to the waxed base can be sponged off. Any finger or tong marks on a piece can be touched up with a small brush after dipping.

 TIPS

Before you dip, be sure the container holds plenty of glaze and that it is deep enough to submerge your entire piece.

Make sure to stir the glaze well before dipping to keep it at the proper fluidity, to blend the ingredients thoroughly, and to ensure an even coating.

8-41 Wearing protective latex gloves, Johnson grips the dish with dipping tongs, ready for glazing.

 TIP

 Wear gloves while applying glaze to protect your hands and to keep oil from your fingers from marking the exterior—oil spots will repel the glaze.

8-42 a The square dish is submerged in the glaze bucket.

 TIPS

If pinholes appear in a glaze after dipping, let the piece dry a few minutes, then rub the open pinhole with your finger to close it.

Or first dilute your glaze solution with water, sponge on a thin layer, then dip the piece into the glaze for a final glaze coating.

8-43 The submerged dish is pulled out immediately. Johnson says the viscosity of his glaze is like "whipping cream consistency."

8-44 The glazed dish is pulled out of the bucket and held over the container a few seconds to catch extra glaze drips.

 TIP

Sponge off any residue glaze beads that may be left on a waxed base after glazing.

8-45 Johnson sponges the excess glaze that drips from the waxed base. The prong marks left by the dipping tongs are touched up with a brush.

POURING GLAZES

The easiest way to glaze the interior surface of a narrow-necked vase is to **pour** the interior glaze in first (8-46a,b). In this way, you can glaze the inside and avoid splashing the interior glaze onto the outer one—unless you want some of the interior color to splash onto the outside for decoration. Pour the glaze into the vase or bottle, then twirl the ware so that the glaze coats the interior evenly, and as quickly as possible, pour the excess back into the bucket. Pouring is also a good way to apply glaze to the inside of a bowl; first you apply glaze to the exterior, then to the interior. We strongly recommend using gloves or tongs when glazing to protect your hands from glaze materials and also to protect the bisque from oil from your fingers.

The pouring technique can also be used to create decoration. You can pour a glaze over the bisqued clay, leaving some areas free of glaze to appear as the contrasting clay color, or you can pour two or more glazes, using blending or varying colors to create a wide range of effects (8-46c). Combining glazes in this way can be extremely effective as long as the multiple glaze patterns do not become so complex that they overwhelm the form.

If you have not coated the base with wax or water sealer, you will need to sponge off any excess glaze to keep the ware from sticking to the kiln shelf during firing (8-46d).

 TIPS

Pour glaze inside first, holding the ware by its clean, exterior bisque surface. This avoids smudging an exterior glaze.

Use a funnel to pour glaze into a narrow necked vase or bottle form.

a

b

8-46 **a** With a twirling movement, make sure that the glaze coats the entire inside; **b** then, as quickly as possible, pour the extra glaze back into the bucket. Wear gloves when pouring glazes.

c

To be sure that a pot does not stick to the kiln shelf, either wax or thoroughly damp sponge both the bottom of the pot and a short way up the outside.

8-46 **c** Although potter Bill Cravis is not wearing gloves in the photos, it is always best to wear them or use tongs when glazing to protect your hands. Pouring two or more glazes can create decorative effects. Experience will teach you how to apply them. **d** It is extremely important to wipe glaze off the bottom of a pot, especially if you have not painted wax on the base. If the glaze is a runny one, you may also need to wipe a short way up the outside of the base, especially if you have not used wax on the base. If any glaze clings to the bottom, the pot may stick to the kiln shelf during firing.

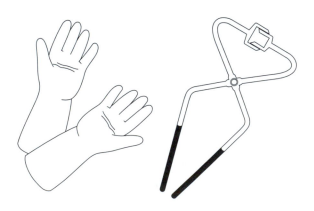

d

SPRAYING GLAZES

It is safest to apply a sprayed glaze in a **spray booth,** wearing a respirator (8-47b). A **spray gun** is extremely useful for coating a pot or sculpture with glazes, oxides, or stains. Some potters prefer to apply glazes by brushing, dipping, or pouring because of the particular effects those methods create. For others, spraying is preferable because using a spray gun is the fastest way to cover the entire surface. Spraying can give a smoother coating than brushing, which may leave distracting lines, lumps, or ridges due to uneven application. Spraying is also a good way to apply glaze over freshly painted oxides, stains, slips, or underglazes that would be likely to smudge if they were glazed with a brush. Before spraying, glazes should be thinned and also sieved so that they will not clog the spray-gun orifice (8-47a).

If you want to do detail spraying or shading with oxides or underglaze, you will need to use an **airbrush.** An airbrush is good for highlighting or accenting glazed areas on a pot or sculpture. You can accent a piece by airbrushing underglazes or oxides on greenware or bisque or by airbrushing them on top of a glaze before firing.

8-47 **a** Frans Duckers, the Netherlands, applies oxides and stains with brushes and sponges to color his sculpture. He finishes it by spraying the surface with thin layers of matt-white and transparent glaze to bring out the oxide color and the color of the clay. He is using a gravity-feed spray gun. *(Courtesy the artist. Photo: Veronique Jean.)* **b** A spray booth not only protects the user but also creates the proper draft to pull the glaze around the piece so that it is applied more evenly. **c** A siphon-feed spray gun.

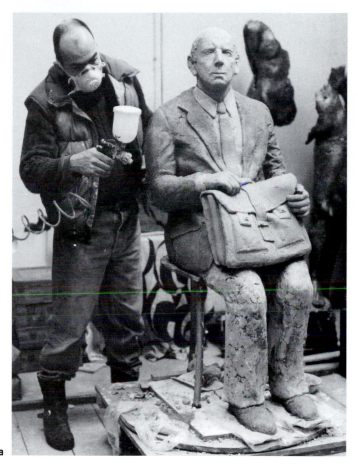

a

b

c

SURFACE TREATMENTS

8-48 *Window Cup* by Ron Nagle. Nagle uses many layers of glazes and china paint, and often decals, to create an evocative surface on his cast porcelain cup forms. Ht 2½ in. (6.35 cm). *Courtesy the artist and Crocker Museum, Sacramento, California. Photo: Ira Schrank. © 1993 Ron Nagle.*

8-49 High-fired wheel-thrown vessel by Robert Brady, who was influenced by Mimbres pottery (8-5) and the asymmetry of Japanese ceramics. Using brushed-on oxide, Brady reinterprets the spirit of the ancient pottery in a contemporary manner. Stoneware. *Courtesy the artist.*

RESIST METHODS

Resist decoration is accomplished by glazing the ware with a base color, blocking off an area with some type of resist, then covering the entire surface with another slip or glaze (Color Plate 23). When this is done, the original color of the clay, slip, or glaze underneath will be visible on the fired piece (8-25, 8-50). The most commonly used resist method employs a commercially available petroleum-based solution, called **wax resist,** but you can also use latex resist, paper stencils (8-25), or masking tape (8-52) to create resist areas. Charles Spacey uses masking tape and wax resist methods to develop his patterned surfaces (Color Plate 12).

If you want your design to come out sharp and clear when you use a wax resist, clean off any excess beads of glaze that remain on the resist, using a damp sponge for cleaning large areas and a small damp brush to clean out glaze left in the detail. On the other hand, for aesthetic reasons, you may want to let these accidental effects remain—as did Shoji Hamada, who often left the glaze residue on the wax and let it fire into his pieces (8-51). You can also combine sgraffito with the wax-resist method by applying a wax coating over a base color, letting it dry, then scratching your design through the wax. After brushing off any wax or glaze residue, sponge or brush a contrasting oxide into the lines. After firing, the lines will show the color of the oxide. Dona Bruhl creates her hard-edge decoration with masking tape (8-51).

 TIP

A removable resist solution can be made by diluting latex 30 to 50 percent with water. Paint on one or two coats, let it dry, glaze your ware, and peel off any unwanted latex resist.

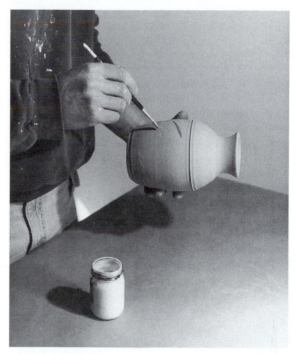

a

b

8-50 a Wax resist is painted onto a blue-glazed vase. The vase will be set aside for ten to fifteen minutes to let the wax dry. **b** The vase has been dipped partway in a bucket of white glaze. Notice that the glaze has not clung to the areas where the wax resist was painted.

8-51 The famous Japanese potter Shoji Hamada used a wax-resist method to decorate this stoneware vase around 1931. Hamada, a Japanese National Treasure, spent a lifetime dedicated to producing beautiful pots that were influenced by Japanese folk pottery. He also was influential in interpreting the Japanese aesthetic to Westerners. *© V & A Picture Library.*

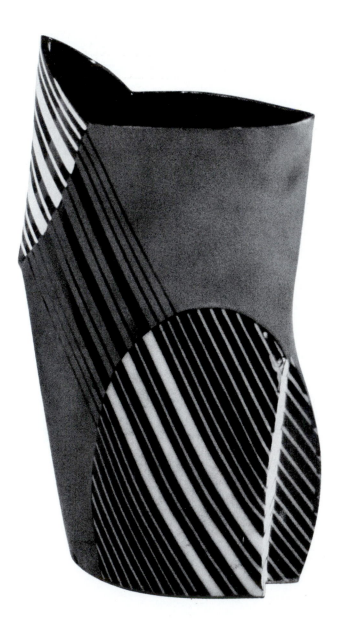

TIP

Thin wax resist slightly with water to make it flow more easily.

8-52 Donna Bruhl, USA, used resist in a hard-edged style in her *Spinnaker Series.* When creating this series of white earthenware slab vessels, she used engobes, stains, underglazes, and commercial glazes for their various surface effects. She sprayed these on with an airbrush over masking tape to make the stripes. On some of the pieces, she also sandblasted certain areas after firing to give them a soft, satiny surface that contrasts with the glaze (Color Plate 23). *Courtesy the artist.*

CHINA PAINTS, OVERGLAZES, AND ENAMELS

Once associated with table china, **china paints, overglazes,** and **enamels** are popular today with both potters and sculptors for the wide range of colors and effects that can be achieved with them. The term *china paint* is often referred to as an overglaze or enamel. These paints are very-low-fire glazes (020 to 016) (1175°F/635°C to 1458°F/792°C) and are usually applied on top of an already glaze-fired surface. If it is applied to a gloss glaze, the china paint will become glossy. If it is applied to a dull or matt surface, the paint will tend to fire matt. China paints can also be applied to unglazed high-fired porcelain surfaces. This method is common when painting porcelain dolls, such as cheeks, or details such as eyes and lips. The term *enamel* refers to opaque overglaze colors while *china paint* refers to translucent overglazes. One real advantage to using china paints is the range of opacity and color they provide, and the detail that can be achieved with them.

China paints, overglazes, and enamels can be applied on top of a fired glaze or porcelain surface with a brush, airbrush, or spray gun, a silk screen, or as a decal except on unglazed porcelain. They are the last firing on ceramics because the firing temperature is well below the maturing point of most base glazes. If the paints are applied in layers to create added depth to a surface (8-48), then separate firings may be necessary to avoid contaminating other colors. For example, bright reds and oranges are easily contaminated by other paints if they are applied next to an unfired color. So it may be best to fire other colors first, then the reds and oranges.

The paints are available commercially in pre-mixed oil-based form, and water color pans, and a wide range of colors in dry powder form. The powders are blended with a special oil medium or water-based vehicle. China paints, overglazes, and enamels offer the ceramist a broad spectrum of colors to explore their potential.

Luster (also **lustre**) is a decorative method developed centuries ago, used to great effect in the Muslim world on both vessels and tiles. Traditional luster technique involves painting metallic salts onto opaque tin glaze, then firing it in a heavily reducing atmosphere in the kiln to develop the color and iridescence of the metallic overglaze.

Today there are some potters who have mastered the art of firing traditional lusters (Color Plate 5), but now commercially prepared lusters are available ready-dissolved in oils that provide a reducing agent so that the ware can be fired in an oxidation atmosphere. Both translucent and opaque lusters are available in a palette of shades, and there are even pens that make it possible to draw or write fine lines with luster. These modern lusters have led artists to experiment with luster, sometimes painting translucent luster on colored glazes so that the glaze color shows through, or even painting luster onto unglazed clay surfaces.

The techniques and processes shown in this chapter are a few of the possible ways you can decorate or enhance the surface of your pottery or sculpture. Chapter 9 will explain how firing affects the various types of ceramic decoration.

KEY TERMS

sprigging	fluxes
burnishing	matt glaze
terra sigillata	sieve
rib	dipping
bisque firing	pouring
engobe	spray booth
slip	spray gun
terra-cotta	airbrush
slip trailer	resist decoration
frit	wax resist
terra sigillata	china paint
oxide	overglazes
stain	enamel
glaze	luster

CREATIVE EXERCISES

1. Make a slab plate (using a hump or press mold) about 10 to 14 in. (25 to 36 cm) in diameter. Decorate the greenware with an oxide or a combination of oxides. Use personal symbols, such as your monogram, political, religious, or spiritual iconography, numerology, or Tarot card symbols. Bisque-fire the oxide-decorated plate, glaze it with a transparent glaze, and fire it to maturity (see Chapter 9).

2. With the help of a mirror, sketch your face; then, from the sketches, create a portrait that reveals an aspect of your character. Imagine that you are making a portrait to be kept in a museum. Bisque-fire it, then use slips, engobes, oxides, and/or glazes to emphasize that aspect of your character.

NOTES/SKETCHES

Firing

Now you have come to the final, and most transforming, aspect of the ceramic process: the **firing** that permanently changes clay from a raw earth material to a new substance—a ceramic object that is produced through the technical expertise and sensitivity of a potter or sculptor. After you have made a number of pots or sculptures, and the **greenware** you have produced has been dried thoroughly, your work is ready to be bisque fired. You may have participated already in a kiln loading and firing cycle. If not, now is the time to familiarize yourself with all aspects of firing, including how to prepare your work for the kiln, the various types of kilns (9-1 to 9-6), and what kind of results each type of kiln produces. You need to get to know the essential parts of a kiln, how it operates, and what controls and monitors its temperature (9-7 to 9-10). You should also observe how the **kiln furniture** is stacked and the ware is loaded in the kiln (9-6, 9-11, 9-12, 9-13, 9-14, 9-22). In addition, it is time for you to understand what happens to clay and glaze

in the kiln as the heat mounts over a period of time, passing through a number of changes, bringing the ware to maturity (Color Plate 30).

In the past, technical information on firing was developed through centuries of experimentation by potters who had no theoretical knowledge of chemistry or thermal engineering. They had to depend on their common sense to work out why a certain design of kiln did not work while another produced successful firings, and they had to depend on experience and intuition to learn how to change a clay body or glaze so that it would fire more successfully. In many parts of the world, including China, Japan, Europe, and the American Southwest, this knowledge has been handed down through generations of potters. In other parts of the world, unfortunately, much of the early tradition has been lost, although archeologists have recently been able to learn a great deal about early clay bodies and firing methods by using modern scientific tests on excavated ceramic ware.

HISTORY

The first step toward a ceramics history was taken when humans tamed fire. Probably the first deliberate ceramic firings were done in **pit** (or **open**) **firing** where the ware was stacked and combustible material piled over and around the pots. Perhaps a low hearth of stone was built around it to contain the fire, or maybe a baffle was built to protect the ware from wind that could make the fire burn erratically. Or firing may have been done in a shallow pit dug into the earth (9-1).

The next development, and none of these were chronological or occurred simultaneously in all areas of the world, was more elaborate kilns that took advantage of the natural upward flow of heat (9-2). Observation would have led early potters to design kilns with increased draft that would in turn cause hotter fires. In China and Japan, potters through thousands of years of activity developed large hillside, often multichambered, *climbing* kilns (9-4). In Europe the basic Mediterranean **updraft kiln** (9-3, 9-4b) was modified and refined for specialized use.

When, in any area of the world, fabrication of domestic ware became an industry, kilns became huge, pouring wood or coal smoke over the pottery-making areas of Asia, England, and Europe. The comparatively recent (nineteenth to twentieth century) development of gas and electricity as fuel was a great improvement, and along with better and less polluting fuel, the ability to monitor and control the kiln was refined. Now, computerized kilns (9-11) largely tend themselves—but the careful potter checks periodically, especially near the end of the firing.

Despite these developments in firing technology, many ceramists have returned to modifications of Japanese wood-burning *anagama* kilns (9-36), *raku* kilns (9-27 to 9-34), pit firing, or postfiring smoking in order to enhance the surfaces of their ware (9-28).

9-3 A Cretan kiln today. Such updraft kilns and their modifications were used for centuries throughout the Mediterranean area and Europe. The ware was set on perforated floors over firing chambers, and the kilns were stoked through a tunnel. Updraft kilns were eventually improved so that they could produce high-fired ware. *Drawing by John M. Casey, based on author's observation and information in the article "The Potters of Thrapsano," by Maria Voyatzoglou, in* Ceramic Review *(November–December 1973).*

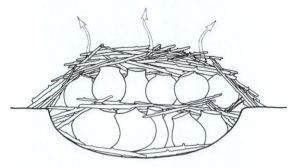

9-1 By observing continuing traditions in indigenous cultures, archeologists deduce that early ceramics were fired on the open ground or in shallow pits, with dried grasses, wood, dung, and peat piled around, in, and over them. Such pit firings produce only low-fired earthenware. *Drawing by John M. Casey.*

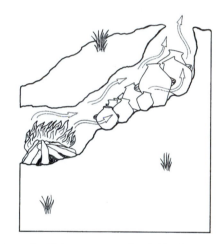

9-2 In early China, potters dug hillside tunnel kilns in which the heat from the wood fire at the bottom of the kiln rose through the ware, creating increased draft and heat. Later improvements led to high-firing kilns. *Drawing by John M. Casey.*

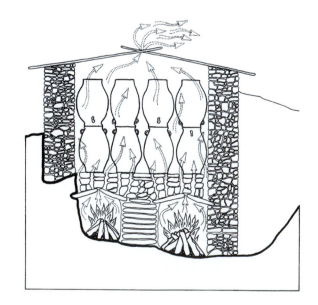

9-4 **a** This drawing shows how the heat flowed through a multichambered hillside kiln. Such kilns were used in China and Japan to fire the huge quantities of ware made for export to Europe. To fire glazed porcelain, such as the blue and white ware so coveted in Europe, the potters would place it in protective containers, called **saggers. b** A basic European updraft kiln design. For clarity, the drawing shows only three pots, but the kiln would have been stacked full of ware on kiln shelves or on columns of bricks. Some kilns had baffles (**bag walls**) that would somewhat protect the ware from the flames and ashes. *Drawings by John M. Casey.*

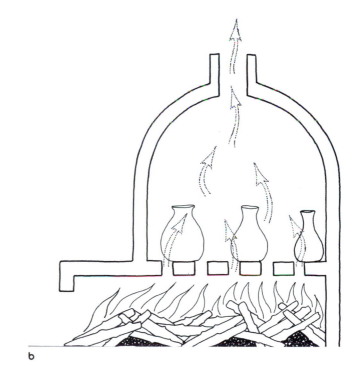

WHAT HAPPENS IN THE FIRE

When clays and glazes are subjected to heat, the materials of which they are composed undergo various changes. Some of the most evident changes occur when these compounds are fired to maturity: The clay becomes hard and will no longer dissolve in water, while glazes become glossy hard, creating a moisture-resistant or waterproof coating. Clay also shrinks by about 3 to 5 percent from the wet to dry state and another 2 to 15 percent from the dry greenware state to fired maturity. Organic matter burning out, along with the vapor being forced out, causes the clay particles to move closer together. In general, smooth clay bodies and those fired to higher temperatures will have a higher shrinkage rate than those with additives such as **grog** or sand.

One invisible change that takes place in a clay body, and in glazes, is a phenomenon called **quartz inversion,** which occurs when they are heated in a kiln to between 440°F/ 227°C and 1070°F/577°C. At this point, the **silica** contained in the clay and glaze physically changes in volume and gradually expands due to the transformation of the material in response to the heat.

There are two critical temperature zones when firing clay. In the early stages, clay will blow up at around the boiling point of water (212°F/100°C) if fired too fast and again through quartz inversion (1070°F/577°C). Solid or extra thick work or damp clay is particularly susceptible to blowing up. If ware is fired too fast, moisture from inside the piece that is turning into steam tries to escape too quickly, causing a buildup of pressure that results in an explosion. For this reason it is particularly important to fire clay slowly through the quartz inversion period (between 212°F/100°C and 1070°F/577°C).

9-5 Peter Coussoulis adjusts the dampers on a gas kiln, which regulates the amount of oxygen or carbon monoxide in the chamber. *Courtesy the artist and the City of Walnut Creek, California, Civic Arts Education Program, Walnut Creek Civic Arts. Photo: David Hanney.*

OXIDATION AND REDUCTION

Although kilns used by ceramists around the world differ in the fuel they use—wood, propane, oil, or cow dung—studio kilns are generally fueled by natural gas or electricity (9-6, 9-7). One important reason gas kilns are used is because they have the ability to achieve an atmosphere called **reduction** (9-20). When the damper is closed down, the amount of oxygen in the kiln is reduced causing incomplete combustion of the fuel. Carbon and carbon monoxide produced from this burning draw oxygen from the materials that form clays and glazes. Under this condition, the oxygen in some minerals is extracted from some clays and glazes causing a chemical change resulting in color changes. For example, a buff-colored clay can turn into a warm orangish color, or a white porcelain can turn into a light gray color.

Electric kilns (9-10), on the other hand, fire with an **oxidation** atmosphere in which there

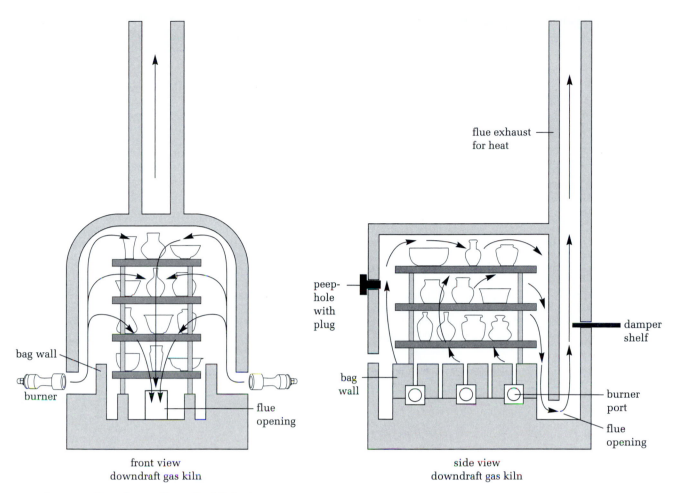

peep-
hole
with
plug

flue exhaust
for heat

damper
shelf

bag
wall

burner
port

flue
opening

bag wall

burner

flue
opening

front view
downdraft gas kiln

side view
downdraft gas kiln

9-6 Cross section of a gas downdraft kiln. In a
downdraft kiln, the heat rises to the top of the kiln,
then is drawn down through the chamber and out
the flue opening at the bottom of the back wall.
This makes for an efficient kiln with an even temperature throughout the interior: The heat remains
in the chamber longer than in updraft kilns in
which the heat rises and goes straight out the top
flue. Arrows show the path of the heat as it goes up
and down, then, finally, out the flue.

is enough free oxygen in the kiln. This is important if you want a clay such as a low-fire
white earthenware or high-fire porcelain to
fire true to color. Glazes fired in an electric
kiln tend to be brighter and clearer, and colors
such as reds and oranges that are sensitive to
kiln temperature variations and to the carbon
of gas kiln atmospheres often fire truer to color
and more consistently when fired in electric
kilns.

Electric kilns are relatively easy to fire, and
in general they fire and cool faster than gas
kilns, which are thick walled and thus hold
heat longer. This means you can complete
work relatively quickly because you can load,

fire, and unload an electric kiln faster than a
gas kiln (9-12). Electric kilns also require less
monitoring than gas kilns, and they are now
available with computers that can be programmed to increase the heat and cool down
the kiln automatically at specific rates, which
makes firings more precise (9-10). This in turn
relieves stresses on clays that are sensitive to
cracking and glazes that might **craze** when the
material is heated through quartz inversion
and then again upon cooling when it reaches
the same critical temperature zone, (around
1070°F/577°C). For the equipment used in firing kilns and the identification of kiln parts,
see Figure 9-7.

KILN FIRING ACCESSORIES

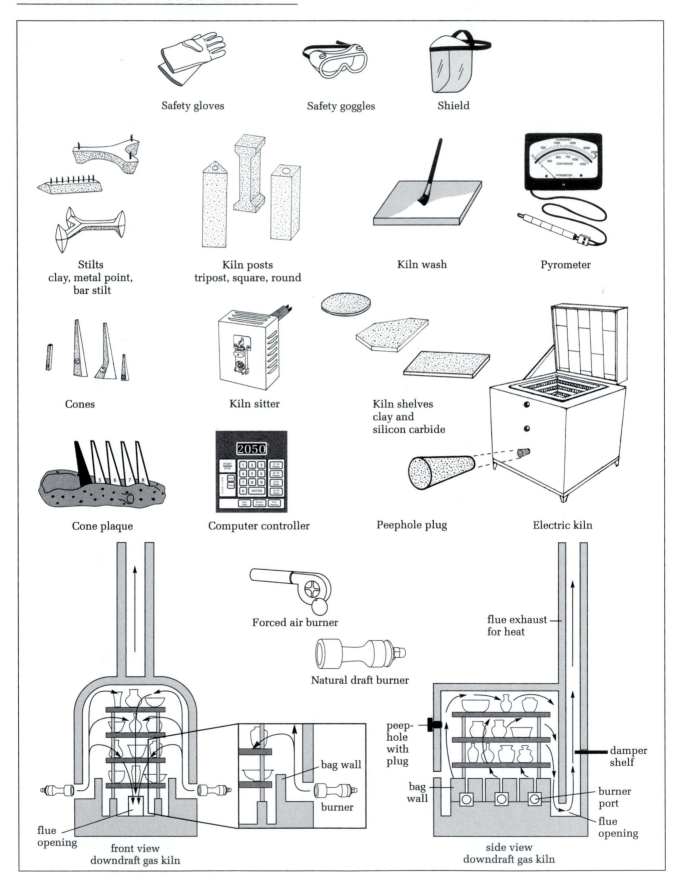

Safety gloves

Safety goggles

Shield

Stilts
clay, metal point,
bar stilt

Kiln posts
tripost, square, round

Kiln wash

Pyrometer

Cones

Kiln sitter

Kiln shelves
clay and
silicon carbide

Cone plaque

Computer controller

Peephole plug

Electric kiln

Forced air burner

Natural draft burner

flue exhaust
for heat

peep-
hole
with
plug

damper
shelf

bag
wall

bag wall

burner

burner
port

flue
opening

flue
opening

front view
downdraft gas kiln

side view
downdraft gas kiln

MONITORING THE KILN

Kiln firing accessories are shown in the chart in 9-7. Tending a kiln requires that the operator monitor various steps and processes. The temperature rise in both electric and gas kilns must be checked carefully to ensure a successful firing since the firing process for most studio kilns takes eight to twelve hours or longer. This is especially crucial at the beginning of firing when ware is susceptible to blowing up or cracking. A **pyrometer** (9-8) is a device that gives you the average temperature inside the kiln and will help you understand what is happening inside the kiln. It lets you know when to lower or close the lid or door of the kiln or when to plug peepholes, turn off dials, or adjust dampers. **Pyrometric cones** (9-9) show you when both the time and the temperature have reached the point at which the clay or glaze has reached maturity.

In modern times, before the advent of computers, both gas and electric kilns were monitored through the use of a series of cones set inside the kiln. They were visually monitored through a peephole until, after many hours, they slumped over, at which point the kiln operator knew it was time to shut off the kiln. This meant that the person firing would frequently have to check on the progression of the kiln by peering through a peephole to see if the cones had fallen.

Later, a kiln sitter (9-10) was developed to automatically shut off an electric kiln, and then became available on small gas kilns to shut off the gas line. A small pyrometric cone was placed inside the kiln on two flat metal bars called Kanthal tips that supported a long metal rod holding a weighted lever in place. Once the cone slumped, the metal rod released a counterweight, which triggered a switch to the kiln, turning off the power.

Today, advanced technology provides computers that give the ceramist greater control over the firing. The kiln can now be programmed and left to fire automatically, simplifying the firing process. Both gas and electric kilns can be operated by computers. Prior to the computer, lids or doors were often left open to vent the kiln during the initial drying periods, and peepholes were needed to view the cones inside. Now, some modern gas kilns have automatic dampers; controlled reduction through special atmospheric monitoring devices; air circulation systems inside the kiln chamber to pre-dry damp ware and lids; and doors and peepholes that remain closed throughout the entire firing. In addition, many kilns are now available with preprogrammed settings to go automatically through the basic firing cycles, similar to operating a microwave oven. Ware fired in such computerized kilns comes out more consistently fired and there are fewer chances of over firing a kiln, or blowing up ware. Fuel is also saved because the kiln remains on only for a specific length of time, and not just when the operator remembers to turn up a switch.

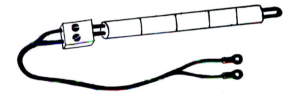

9-8 A pyrometer measures and records the interior temperature of the kiln. The tip of the long probe, called a **thermocouple,** is placed inside the kiln through a small opening. The thermocouple senses the heat and transfers the data to the gauge so that you know when to adjust the kiln controls.

9-9 Pyrometric cones are small pyramids of ceramic materials that are placed inside kilns to help monitor the temperature. They are formulated to bend over at designated temperatures. Cones are available in small or large sizes; the small ones are primarily used in electric kilns and the large ones in gas kilns.

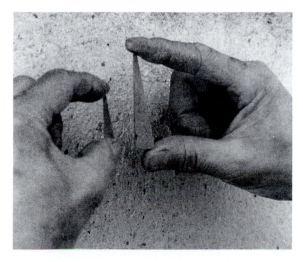

◀ **9-7** This chart acquaints you with the accessories and equipment commonly used in the operation of kilns.

Computers can also be custom programmed to fit the needs of the ware being fired. At the California College of Arts and Crafts, for example, a special computer program is set to bisque fire ware over a period of 45–50 hours; even slightly damp ware has been fired in the kiln, including sculpture as thick as 1¼" (32 mm). The simple one-button operation of the computerized kiln improves all types of firings and makes it easier for beginners to fire. It also saves time for the studio manager who no longer needs to check the kiln four or five times during firing (9-10).

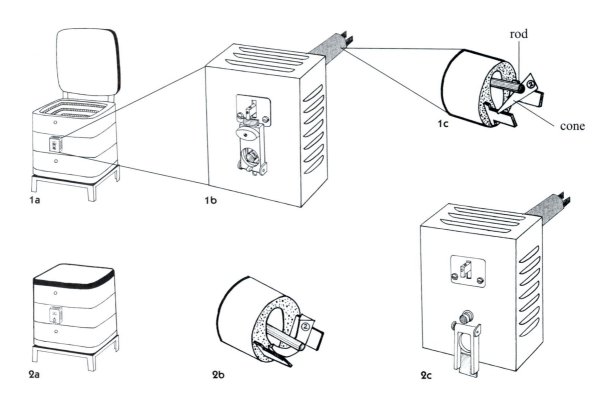

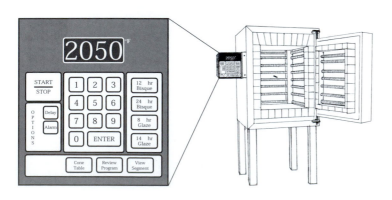

9-10 A modern computerized electric kiln provides excellent heat control, automatically advancing the temperature. Such kilns can also be programmed to "hold" a temperature at a set point, and step down the temperature when cooling. A kiln sitter (1a,b) is a mechanical device attached to a kiln that automatically shuts off the electricity. A thin metal rod (sensing rod) (1c), held up by a small pyrometric cone sits on two flat metal bars (Kanthal tips). To use, place the small cone in the kiln sitter, load the kiln and close the lid (2a). Turn on the kiln, and when it reaches the correct temperature, the cone slumps (2b) into a half moon shape, lowering the sensing rod (2c). This releases a weight that trips an electric switch, shutting off the kiln.

BISQUE FIRING

Generally, dried clay objects are first fired in a **bisque firing** (9-11 to 9-14) in which the dry greenware is heated to beyond the point of quartz inversion (1070°F/577°C) and until it is chemically changed to a hard, dense material. This change usually occurs between cone 010 (1661°F/577°C). Bisque firing serves several purposes: It makes the ware stronger and less likely to break when handled or glazed; if you did not bisque-fire a piece and applied glaze to greenware and fired it too fast, the ware could blow up, causing glazed fragments to stick to the kiln interior and other ware in the kiln. In addition, by bisque firing first, glazes will tend to fire with less **pinholing** and produce brighter colors.

A bisque firing can take up to two to three times longer than a glaze firing because the ware must be heated slowly to drive out all the moisture. Firing a bisque kiln with ware that is ¼ to ⅜ in. (6 to 10 mm) thick takes about nine to fifteen hours. For work ⅝ in. (15 mm) thick, an average firing is sixteen to twenty-four hours or longer. After a kiln has reached the required temperature, the cooling takes between fifteen and twenty-four hours or longer, depending on the size of the kiln. Although ware may appear dry when it is loaded into a kiln, it actually still contains 5 or 6 percent water. For sculptural works up to 1 to 1½ (25 to 38 mm) thick, a bisque firing can take forty to fifty hours to fire and eighteen to thirty-six hours to cool. The thicker the piece, the slower it needs to be fired.

Loading a Bisque Kiln

In a bisque firing, it is safe to let greenware touch the kiln shelves since there is no glaze on the ware, which would cause the ware to stick to the shelves. For the same reason, pots can be stacked inside or on top of each other (9-12 to 9-14). However, if you have odd-shaped pottery or sculpture with protrusions, it is a good idea to pack the kiln loosely; this will lessen the chance of breakage during loading because there is more room to maneuver the pieces. The firing will also be more even, and the air space around the work allows the kiln heat to radiate around the objects more thoroughly, saturating the clay. Firing ware ¼ to ⅜ in. (6 to 10 mm) thick usually takes about nine to fifteen hours. The length of time to fire thicker ware in a bisque firing is also related to the amount of mass inside the kiln; the greater the mass of the load of pottery or sculpture, the longer the firing time will be.

9-11 Bill Cravis loads greenware into an electric kiln for a bisque firing to cone 05 (1915°F/1046°C).

 TIPS

For greater kiln shelf stability, load smaller works in the lower section of the kiln and larger works near the top.

A sparsely packed kiln will fire faster than one that is fully loaded.

9-12   An electric kiln fully loaded with wheel-thrown bowls and tumblers ready for firing to cone 05 (1915°F/1046°C). The bowls are stacked one inside another, rim to rim, or base to base, and the tumblers are loaded on either end of the kiln shelf with each tumbler stacked on the base or rim of another tumbler. This maximizes the full volume of the kiln and reduces the number of kiln shelves and posts required to load the kiln. The ware can touch each other in the bisque firing because there is no glaze to fuse the pieces together.

 TIP

Fire greenware over ¼ in. (6 mm) thick very slowly in the early stages, venting the kiln by leaving the door or lid open 1 to 2 in. (25 to 50 mm) or more, while the kiln is on low heat.

 TIP

Load thick sculptural pieces in the center or upper center of the kiln where the heat is most even.

9-13 Sections of the kiln have been removed to show what a bisque load looks like halfway into the loading. A kiln shelf has also been removed, revealing the three triangular kiln posts in their correct position to support a shelf. For increased stability and support, as shelves are subsequently stacked, it is best to place kiln posts directly above the ones below.

Potter Bill Cravis says,

After loading an electric kiln full of pots, I turn on the bottom switch to low, with the lid propped up 3 inches (8 cm) to let the ware dry out, and warm up overnight. In the morning I touch the ware to see if it is hot. If it is nice and toasty, I lower the lid to 1 inch (2.54 cm) and turn all the switches to low for two hours. Then each hour I turn one switch up until I am at medium. At this point I close the lid and turn the bottom switch to high and continue to turn dials until all switches are on high. I close all the **peephole** *plugs, except the top, and let the kiln fire off which takes about three to four hours to reach 1915 degrees Fahrenheit. I always return to check the kiln shortly after the expected firing time, to make sure it has gone off.*

9-14 Sections of the kiln have been removed so that you can see how the ware is stacked for a bisque firing. The pieces closest to the kiln wall are also spaced about 1 in. (2.54 cm) from the kiln elements in the wall so that the ware does not get too hot too fast.

GLAZE FIRING

A **glaze firing** follows a bisque firing. Since the ware has already been fired, there is no danger that work will blow up during glaze firing; therefore, the glaze firing is usually much faster than the bisque firing.

Any glaze must be cleaned off the bases or feet of pottery or sculpture before ware is placed on kiln shelves. The top side of kiln shelves should be kiln washed to protect them in the event that glaze drips off a pot or sculpture during a firing and ruins a shelf. Low-fire ware that is glazed on the bottom must be **stilted** (9-15) to keep glaze from sticking to kiln shelves.

The length of a glaze firing depends on a number of variables. Many potters fire their glazed ware between six and twelve hours. Sculptors working at a large scale or potters making thick pieces should preheat their work in the kiln overnight and complete the glaze firing the next day. In any case, preheating thick glazed ware or sculpture slowly is best since it lets any moisture from the glaze dry out, reducing heat shock that could cause the clay to crack. For a glaze kiln, cooling usually takes twelve to twenty-four hours, depending on the size of the kiln and its insulating properties, the amount of ware, and the mass of the shelves, bricks, and posts inside the kiln. Some large gas kilns require up to four days to cool, before work can safely be removed without cracking.

 TIP

Be sure all glaze is sponged off the bottom of pottery or sculpture before loading it into a kiln for firing high-fire glazes. If you are loading and firing low-fire pottery or sculpture and have glazed the entire piece, including the foot, be sure to stilt the piece properly.

9-15a Kiln wash brushed onto kiln shelves keeps pottery or sculpture from sticking to the shelves, and also protects the shelves from glaze drips that might stick to them.

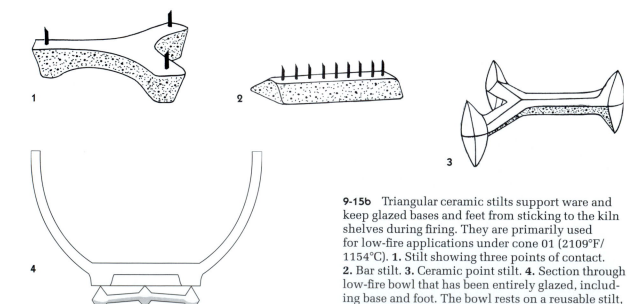

9-15b Triangular ceramic stilts support ware and keep glazed bases and feet from sticking to the kiln shelves during firing. They are primarily used for low-fire applications under cone 01 (2109°F/1154°C). **1.** Stilt showing three points of contact. **2.** Bar stilt. **3.** Ceramic point stilt. **4.** Section through low-fire bowl that has been entirely glazed, including base and foot. The bowl rests on a reusable stilt, which will keep it from sticking to the kiln shelf.

9-16 Before and after photograph of large pyrometric cones inserted into a clay pad, called a cone pad. **a** The cones are set at an 18-degree angle with the cones placed in a row from left (lowest bending cone) to right (highest bending cone) in the order in which they will slump. **b** The fired cone pad shows the slumped cones after a firing. The white depression on the pad marks the firing cone; when this cone melts, the correct temperature has been reached. The kiln is turned off when the firing cone bends.

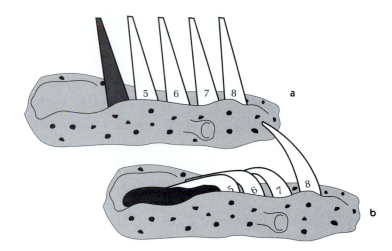

9-17 a Ross Spangler places cones in his gas-fired updraft kiln. The ware was bisque-fired in an electric kiln before being loaded for the glaze firing. **b** The glaze firing lasted eleven hours with a six-hour reduction to get good copper red colors. Now the glaze firing is completed and the kiln is open, displaying a load of glazed bowls, plates, and vases.

a

b

9-18 High-fired stoneware tumblers spaced ³⁄₁₆–¼ in. (4–6 mm) apart to keep the glazed pots from sticking to each other demonstrates the appropriate distance between pieces when glaze firing. During the firing process, glaze volatilizes and often bubbles up, causing the ware to stick if loaded too close to each other. Since the tumblers have no glaze on their feet, they were loaded directly on the kiln shelf.

9-19 A glazed tumbler on the right after firing, and a similar piece before firing, shows the shrinkage of the clay and change in color at the base of the foot as a result of the gas-fired reduction atmosphere. It also shows the transformation of a glaze after firing into a glossy, mottled surface.

TRANSFORMATION

The glaze firing process (9-18 to 9-21) can provide magical moments, such as when you peer through a peephole wearing a shaded safety shield to watch the chamber turn from dark cherry red in the beginning to orange to bright white as the temperature increases. In gas kilns there is a gentle roar as gas burners are turned up and the kiln gets hotter. Cones will start bending (9-16) letting you know the firing is nearly complete. Through a peephole, you can watch glazes on a pot or sculpture attain a glistening melted look when the ware is reaching maturity. While heat and the time spent in the kiln can transform ceramics into wondrous objects, the results can be different with each firing because of the fluctuations in the kiln temperature from top to bottom. In addition, the ware will shrink in size—up to 20 percent of its original size—as it is heated to higher and higher temperatures and the glaze compounds fuse together to form matt or lustrous surfaces.

OXIDATION AND REDUCTION ATMOSPHERES

9-20 A porcelain plate by Catharine Hiersoux. The bold brush design on the plate is offset by the elegant glazed white porcelain background and is achieved with various glazes and a copper-red glaze splash. It was fired in a gas kiln under a reduction atmosphere to attain the reddish colors. Diam. 18 in. (46 cm). *Courtesy the artist. Photo: Richard Sargent.*

9-21 A teapot with a striking black cross pattern by Sandy Simon. The piece was clear glazed over porcelain, with black glaze stain, and fired to cone 6 in an electric kiln. 8 × 6 × 5 in. (20 × 13 × 15 cm). *Courtesy the artist. Photo: Joe Schopplin.*

9-22 An updraft kiln loaded with a large sphere, by Michelle Kern, ready for unloading. The kiln was fired under a reduction atmosphere to enhance the earthy richness of the clay and the underglazed surface. The kiln shelves were supported with heavy-duty kiln posts to add stability, and extra bricks cradled the piece so that it would not roll. Fired to cone 06 (1830°F/999°C).

9-23 Sadashi Inuzuka's *Spirit Boats*, a series of six ceramic vessels positioned in an order based on an imaginary procession of boats floating down a stream. The decorative imagery on the pieces was inspired by Inuzuka's fascination with designs, shapes, and patterns related to insects. Length: 5 ft (1.53 m). Light reduction in gas kiln. *Courtesy the European Ceramics Work Center, the Netherlands.*

HISTORICAL RAKU

Raku firing developed in Japan in the sixteenth century as an adjunct to the Zen tea ceremony. The word *raku* traditionally belongs only to ware made by members of a Japanese family who were given permission to use the character *raku* (pleasure) to identify their ware. Their ware was thick walled and heavy, handbuilt by pinching and carving, without joins. Since the ware was subjected to intense shock when it was placed in and taken out of a red-hot kiln, a seamless pot was practical. Uneven and simple in shape, with accidental surface effects from the fire, the tea bowls were valued as much for how they felt in the hands as how they looked when filled with frothy green tea (9-24)

CONTEMPORARY RAKU

As raku is used in the West today, however, the word refers to a wide range of techniques which have been so modified from the traditional methods that early Japanese practitioners would hardly recognize the Western techniques as raku (9-25 to 9-35). Innovations like modern, ready-made raku kilns, brightly colored, low-fire glazes, and the various chemical additives and compounds, such as silver nitrate and bismuth subnitrate, that potters now use to produce lustrous glazed and fired surfaces were totally unknown to the early raku masters. In addition, nontraditional raku usually involves various methods of reduction and **postfiring fuming** (or smoking).

9-24 A classic Japanese raku tea bowl carved in one piece, not thrown or coiled. The lip, the "tea pool" in the bottom, and the interior spiral that leads tea to the drinker's mouth were all regulated by strict rules. The irregular shape of the bowl and the glaze result in a dynamic aesthetic union. Raku, earthenware with black-brown glaze. Japan, seventeenth century A.D. © *V & A Picture Library.*

9-25 A raku wall plate by Skip Esquierdo. The strong geometry of the black bands adds definition to the overall design and interacts with the ethereal qualities of the variegated raku-glazed surface and low-relief sculpted forms. Esquierdo says, *My plates are a combination of design and surface treatment. I am interested in developing glaze finishes . . . to create new and interesting surfaces that work with the design of the plate. . . . Glazes range from raku to cone 06 and cone 07 commercial glazes.* 13 × 17 in. (33 × 43 cm). *Courtesy the artist. Photo: Lee Fatheree.*

GLAZES FOR RAKU

We recommend that until you gain sufficient experience, you let your supervisor load and fire the kiln.

To prepare your ware for raku firing, it is important to use a clay that is formulated to stand the quick heating and cooling of the raku process. A coarse clay tends to crack less than a smooth or fine-grained one, and a white clay will give your glazes a wider range of colors and truer tones than a dark one. Your ware must be well made, with walls and feet that are not too thin, and if it is handbuilt the seams must be properly scored and tightly joined. Delicate attachments such as handles are susceptible to breakage during handling and require extra care in the firing process, so—at least at first—make simple forms without appendages. It is also a good idea to keep them small until you fully understand the process of raku firing and know what can happen in the firing. All ware should first be bisque fired to the recommended temperature for the clay you are using—generally from cone 015 (1479°F/804°C) to cone 05 (1915°F/1046°C).

Appropriate temperatures for raku firing range from about cone 015 to 05, so make sure you use a glaze with a maturing temperature within that low range. Remember that the appearance of the finished piece will be influenced by such factors as the thickness of the glaze and the manner in which it is applied, as well as by whatever combination of glazes you may have used. Results will also be affected by the heat to which the ware is fired and by the combustible materials used to reduce the glaze after the ware has been removed from the kiln.

Most potters have favorite glazes they have developed for use in raku firing. To experience the entire raku process from glaze testing to fired pot, you may want to mix the following glaze, then apply it on a small pot or test tile in your first raku firing.

RAKU GLAZE: CLEAR CRACKLE

Cone 05 (1915°F/1046°C)

VOLUME	WEIGHT	
6 tablespoons Frit 25	45.0	gm
2 tablespoons Nepheline Syenite	16.0	gm
1½ tablespoons EPK China clay (Kaolin)	8.0	gm
1 teaspoon Bentonite	2.0	gm
6 tablespoons water	64.0	gm

YIELD: 3 fluid ounces (89 mL)

Blend the materials together with water in a cup. Pour the mixture into a mortar and grind with a pestle for two or three minutes until the mixture is smooth and creamy, without lumps. Or mix the glaze and sieve it through an 80 mesh sieve.

COLORANTS to test in above mixture: Divide into three 1-tablespoon batches. The glaze mixed above yields about 8 tablespoons of glaze.

ADD one color to each of the separated batches.

COLORANTS BY VOLUME	WEIGHT
Cobalt oxide (blue) 1 pinch (¹⁄₁₆ teaspoon)	0.25 gm
Copper Oxide (green) 1 pinch (¹⁄₁₆ teaspoon)	0.25 gm
#6443 Praseodymium stain (yellow) 2 pinches (⅛ teaspoon)	1.00 gm

1 pinch equals approximately ¹⁄₁₆ teaspoon

Note: For the most accurate results it is best to weigh out the chemicals on a gram scale.

Measure out the chemicals into a small cup and blend while dry. Next add the water and stir the mixture until it becomes a smooth, creamy consistency. Paint two or three coats on a test tile or pot and place it in the raku kiln and fire to cone 05 (1915°F/1046°C).

To add color to the glaze, add one pinch of cobalt for blue, one pinch of copper oxide for turquoise blue, and eleven pinches of red iron

9-26 In *Viaje Despues de la Vida* (*The Voyage to the Afterlife*), Jack Thompson created a sculpture that combines the Japanese raku-firing technique with Egyptian and indigenous American images—symbolic of the many influences at work in ceramics today. Egyptian blue glaze on the figure of Anubis and the interior of the vessel-figure. 1992. 8 × 19 × 4 in. (20 × 48 × 10 cm). *Courtesy the artist.*

oxide for straw brown. Experiment with this recipe, changing the colorants, testing to see what happens in the kiln and in the postfiring reduction. The variations of color you will achieve in the firing are based on the quantity of colorants added, the clay type, the firing temperature, the fuel used in the firing, and the reducing material such as pine needles or newspaper.

To experience the immediacy of the glaze transformation in a raku kiln, you can peer into the firing chamber wearing a safety shield and see the glaze melt into a glossy surface. Once the glaze turns to a bright orange and is mature—showing a smooth, glassy surface—the ware can be removed from the kiln with tongs and immediately plunged into a metal container filled with some form of flammable material such as shredded newspaper, pine needles, dry leaves, straw, or excelsior. Skip Esquierdo reverses the usual reducing steps by placing a metal container *over* his pots instead of plunging the pots *into* a can of combustible reducing material. In a dirt pit, on a wooden board, he prepares a small pile of dry pine

needles. When the pot is red hot he removes it from the kiln with tongs and sets the piece on a thin layer of pine needles, and also places a handful of needles on the shoulder of the pot. He then quickly covers the pot, board, and needles with a metal bucket. Esquierdo says the board keeps the pot from falling over preventing pine needles from scarring the red-hot glazed surface (9-27). If you participate in this postfiring fuming part of the process, be prepared for a sudden flare-up of flame when the heat of the ware ignites the material. Cover the container, and be patient! Give your ware at least 15 minutes to smoke and cool off before you lift the lid. The ware will still be hot, so continue to wear your heat-reistant gloves and use tongs when you handle it.

Finally, don't be disappointed that your pot comes out sooty and covered with ash. This is normal. Some potters leave some of the soot on the ware for aesthetic reasons, but if you prefer not to do so, scrubbing off the firing residue with a brush and scouring powder will reveal the full color and texture of the raku piece.

9-27 After putting the pot on the plywood, Esquierdo places a handful of pine needles on the top of the red-hot pot. This part of the process must be done very quickly so that the needles will ignite and create the reduction he wants for his pot.

9-28 Esquierdo quickly places a bucket over the smoking pot and needles. He then pulls the earth up around the base of the bucket to seal the smoke in. This not only helps create the reduction atmosphere, it also makes for an almost smokeless raku firing.

9-29 After about one-half hour, Esquierdo removes one of his pots from under its bucket and examines the surface the raku firing and reduction have created.

9-30 A portable raku kiln fueled with propane. The kiln burner system is equipped with a safety shut-off valve that shuts the kiln off in the event the flame is blown out by the wind. A high-pressure regulator on the tank stem provides consistent pressure and uniform flow of fuel going into the burner. A pressure gauge attached to the regulator on the propane tank stem provides accurate readings of the gas pressure.

There is drama and excitement in the contemporary raku process as you plunge the red-hot ware into some form of combustible material for reduction, but participation in the process is also an opportunity to see quickly what happens to glaze in the fire (9-35). Raku allows nuance and personal touches, and it often provides exciting results. Despite its apparent simplicity, however, it is not an elementary technique, and beginners should follow these safety procedures:

- **Fire a raku kiln only under the supervision of an experienced person.**
- Wear face mask and eye protection, long sleeves, long, heavy pants, and high-top leather boots when you place your ware in the reduction can. Do not wear synthetic clothing, which may be flammable.
- Tie back long hair when working around the kiln.
- Use long non-asbestos heat-resistant gloves and tongs.
- Have a water supply such as a hose readily available.
- Keep the area around the kiln clear of combustibles.
- Exercise great care when removing ware and plunging it into combustible material.
- Keep flammable material away from hot ware.
- Wear a respirator rated for toxic fumes when reducing.

9-31 Skip Esquierdo loads one of his wall plates into his raku kiln, carefully propping it in a tilted position. This allows the heat to flow more evenly around the plate and helps to keep the plate from cracking in the firing. (See also Color Plate 22.)

9-32 Loading the first of the glazed ware in the kiln. Because the kiln is cold, the ware can be loaded without fear of it cracking, and there is no need to wear gloves. The first firing of a raku kiln usually reaches about 1900°F (1038°C).

9-33 For this loading, heat-resistant gloves are essential because after the first firing, the kiln will be hot. The ware for subsequent firings must be preheated on top of the kiln lid while an earlier load is firing; this lessens the shock of the heat on the pottery, which could cause cracking. Note the water hose, which should always be kept handy when postfiring reduction is done.

9-34 Skip Esquierdo removes a pot from his raku kiln. The kiln is an electric kiln stripped of its elements and turned into a raku kiln through the use of a propane gas burner inserted in the bottom of the kiln. A hole in the lid serves as a vent. A piece of plywood is ready to support the pot in the dirt in his reduction pit.

9-35 Sebastian Hushbeck was inspired by the natural surroundings of Washington state when he made this raku vase. In throwing pots and raku-firing his work, he says his fascination is with *"the dichotomy between the controlled methods of the wheel, and the immediacy and spontaneity of the raku process."* Courtesy the artist. Photo: Guy Nicol.

Finally, be aware of and respect the traditional aspects of the raku process even though you may use it in a completely contemporary and experimental manner. Raku expert Steve Branfman says,

to trivialize a process with as long a chronology and as many variations as raku would do a great injustice to our craft. Raku is a wonderful way to be involved in clay as long as you keep an honest perspective on your experience, intentions, and goals.

WOOD FIRING

Wood firing has a long history; Chinese and Japanese potters became experts in building wood-firing kilns that they used to create glazed ware of great beauty. In the West, wood firing has become newly popular with many contemporary potters such as Richard Carter of Napa, California, now building Japanese-style wood kilns (9-36). As a result, wood firing has acquired a rather romantic reputation, but to the early potter it was pure necessity due to the lack of any other fuel. Until gas and electricity were used for heating kilns, wood and in unforested areas, other natural materials such as peat or dried dung, were the only fuel available.

During the combustion of the wood the varying minerals that exist in the fuel can interact with minerals in the clay and form an **ash** glaze. Wood firing, which requires constant stoking during the firing period, can produce surprising results—the ashes in the kiln can affect any applied slips and glazes, producing variations in glazes, and also may create unexpected flashes of color.

9-36 Two views of an Anagama style kiln built by Richard Carter. He uses pine and poplar wood to fuel his kiln, which he fires to cone 12. The ash from the wood reacts with the clay, naturally forming a glaze. *Courtesy the artist. Photo: Bonita Cohn.*

SALT-GLAZING

Salt-glazing was first developed along the Rhine valley in Germany in the early sixteenth century where it was widely used on stoneware to give it an impermeable surface. The technique spread to England and later to the American colonies where it was used on storage pots as well as jugs. The glaze was unaffected by the brine or vinegar used to preserve foods in stoneware crocks before the use of refrigeration.

The development of a salt glaze depends on the amount of silica in the clay body, and the ware must be heated to a high temperature before the added sodium combines with the silica of the clay to produce a transparent glaze.

Ben Owen, for example, heats his kiln to (2350°F/1288°C) before he introduces the salt (9-39a,b, Color Plate 29a,b).

Because of the environmental impact of salt firing, a number of potters have developed various recipes for cutting down on the amount of salt in the formula as well as the amount of hydrochloric acid released by earlier salt kilns.

Whatever method or fuel you use to fire your ware, the process is the culmination of the ceramic process, bringing clay and fire together, creating the interaction that transforms your pot or sculpture—sometimes in unexpected ways. This transformation is one of the most compelling aspects of pottery making, and even the most experienced ceramist responds to the excitement of opening a kiln.

9-37 *Memory,* by Richard Carter, is a twelve panel wall piece that captures the essence of the human spirit. Carter utilizes elements of the figure, and text, which adds to the emotional qualities of the piece. He carefully places chemicals in his sculptural works that interact with the wood ash during firing creating unique surface colors and texture. His understanding of how and where the wood ash falls on his work is part of the firing aesthetic. Carter says, *I am interested in "pushing the limits" of the traditional wood fired process through the use of various chemical additives.* 48 × 60 in. (122 × 152 cm). Stoneware, found objects, silica rock, oxides. Fired to cone 12. *Photo: Stefan Kirkeby.*

PROFILE Ben Owen

Potter Ben Owen III forms his pottery on the wheel and often fires it with wood, using salt vapor to glaze it. Both these firing techniques are ancient, but Owen works in a modern studio and fires his work in an updated wood kiln, as well as using gas and electric kilns.

Nevertheless, tradition is strong in his family; his potting forefathers came from England as early as 1756 and set up their workshops in the area of North Carolina where Ben Owen III's pottery is located. These early potters, drawn by the local sources of clay, supplied storage jars and other utilitarian pottery for the use of neighboring farmers. In the 1920s, their descendent, the first Ben Owen, who was also the son of a potter, joined with Jacques Busbee to develop the later-famous Jugtown Pottery. There they produced traditional pottery, but when Busbee got in touch with the Tiffany Studios in New York and arranged for them to distribute the pottery, Tiffany's encouraged the two to try new forms, new glazes.

Han vase, by Ben Owen. Like his potter father and grandfather, Ben Owen III searches for simplicity of form and decoration. Although Owen uses both gas and electric kilns, he still likes to fire with wood for the aesthetic effects. Stoneware, sprayed oxides. Wood fired, then salt-glazed. Ht. 12 in. (30 cm).

By the time Ben Owen Sr. opened his own workshop, the influence of the ancient Chinese and Japanese pottery he and Busbee had studied in museums led him to redesign and refine the forms and to develop a wider range of glazes. His son, Ben Owen Jr., originally a political science teacher, helped during vacations, learned pottery skills, glazed and fired ware, and later ran the pottery.

Thus, when Ben Owen III was born in 1968, he grew up surrounded by clay, wheels, kilns, and pots. *With hundreds of pots on the shelves of my grandparents' and parents' homes, I wanted to know why these pots were so much a part of their lives, and I asked many questions. . . . I studied each one as a different lesson for the day.* Remembering his study of the pots on the shelves, he says now, *Many of the forms that granddad made were influenced by other cultures: Chinese, Japanese, Korean, Persian as well as early English. Among many cultures my grandfather found a common element of simplicity in form, design, and color. My grandfather often said, "It is easy to make things complicated, but hard to keep things simple." I find it a daily challenge to follow his advice in a world where instant gratification is a common expectation.* With his childhood exposure to the best in pottery, Ben III became seriously interested in ceramics, and his ambition at around twelve was to achieve the title Master Potter like his grandfather had.

(continued)

After high school graduation, an assistantship teaching pottery, and business study, Ben III earned a BFA in ceramics at East Carolina University. There, he expanded his interest in and knowledge of form and color in ceramics, and explored other art media. When he returned to work in the family pottery, many of the Asian-influenced shapes and glazes created by Ben Sr. were still being produced. His grandson continued the family tradition and, after traveling to Japan to be part of a ceramic workshop in Tokoname, he widened the range of form and surface of the ware through his own experience of Japanese ceramics.

Today, Ben Owen III continues to follow the historical tradition of his family, while bringing his personal sensitivity to the pieces he throws and decorates. *It is a challenge,* he says, *to honor my past while creating a vision for the future. All the while, remembering my grandfather's advice, "Keep it simple, Son. Keep it simple."*

Ben Owen III stokes his wood kiln. He says, *Today, I fire with gas and electricity, but still prefer the effects of firing in my wood kiln. The color and texture are affected by the many variables the wood firing presents. Smoke, flame and ash are manipulated to produce various results with each firing.* (See also Color Plate 00 a,b).

YOUR FUTURE IN CLAY

Now that you have tried most of the techniques shown in this book, we hope you will have been captivated by the craft and art of ceramics. If so, you probably have already discovered which methods are most comfortable for you and what areas you'd like to explore further. There is a lifetime of discovery ahead of you and much satisfaction to be derived from mastering at least some of the techniques so that you can use them expertly. Whether you choose to make household pottery or sculpture installations, clay offers you a chance to imprint your own identity on it, to express your deepest feelings or needs, using it with respect and care. In the process, also be careful of your own health and safety and that of the environment around you. Good claying!

KEY TERMS

firing
greenware
kiln furniture
pit (or open) firing
updraft kiln
sagger
bag wall
grog
quartz inversion
silica
reduction

pyrometer
pyrometric cones
thermocouple
bisque firing
peephole
glaze firing
stilts
raku firing
postfiring fuming
wood firing
salt-glazing

NOTES/SKETCHES

Glossary

airbrush An atomizer that uses compressed air to spray a liquid. In ceramics, used for spraying oxides, underglazes, glaze stains, china paint, and lusters.

alkaline glazes Glazes in which the fluxes are alkalies (mainly sodium and potassium). The earliest glazes developed in the Near East were alkaline.

alumina One of the refractory (high-melting) materials in glazes.

armature A framework of any rigid material used as a support while building clay sculpture. Most armatures must be removed before firing.

ashes In ceramics, ashes from trees, plants, or animal bones may provide fluxes for use in glazes.

bag wall A wall built inside a kiln firing chamber to protect the ware from the flame. It sends the flames upward and also helps create even circulation in the kiln.

ball clay A plastic, fine-grained secondary clay. Often containing some organic material, it is used in clay bodies to increase plasticity, and in glazes to add alumina. Ball clay fires to a grayish or buff color.

banding wheel A turntable that can be revolved with one hand to turn a piece of pottery or sculpture while the other hand decorates it.

bas-relief (or low relief) Three-dimensional modeling that is raised only slightly above a flat background.

bat A plaster disk or square slab usually ¾ to 1½ in. (19.05 to 37.5 mm) thick on which a pot is thrown or is placed to dry when removed from the wheel. Also used when handbuilding.

batch A mixture of glaze materials or ingredients that have been blended in certain proportions to obtain a particular glaze or clay body.

bisque (biscuit) Unglazed ceramic ware that has been fired at a low temperature to removed all moisture from the clay body and to make handling easier during glazing.

bisque firing The process of firing ware at a low temperature, usually from cone 010 to 05, to produce bisque ware.

bisque mold A mold made from fired clay. It is low fired around cone 010 to 05 (1661°F/905°C to 1915°F/1046°C) and is generally used as a press mold and for sprigging.

Bizen ware Produced in Japan in wood-fired kilns in which the pots are stacked along with straw that is high in silica content. Its combustion causes fire markings.

body (clay body) Any blend of clays and nonplastic ceramic materials that is workable and that has certain firing properties. Clay bodies are formulated to serve particular purposes and to achieve maturity at various firing temperatures. See **earthenware, stoneware,** and **porcelain.**

body The main structure of a sculpture, or cylindrical core of a pot.

brushing In ceramics, the application of slip, engobe, or glaze with a brush.

burner (gas, propane, or **oil)** The system through which fuel, combined with air, is fed into the kiln, creating the necessary mixture for combustion.

burnishing Rubbing leather-hard or dry clay with any smooth tool to polish it, tighten the clay surface, and compress the clay particles.

casting In ceramics, the process of forming pottery or sculpture by pouring liquid clay (slip) into an absorbent plaster mold.

celadon The Western name for a type of glaze first used in China on stoneware and porcelain in an attempt to imitate the color and texture of jade. Its colors range from shades of green to gray-green tones.

centering   The act of forcing a lump of clay by hand into a symmetrical form at the center of a spinning potter's wheel in preparation for throwing pottery.

centrifugal force   The force generated by a rotating potter's wheel that tends to impel the clay outward from the center of the wheel head. The action of the potter's hands in conjunction with this force causes the wall to rise.

ceramics   Objects made from earthy materials with the aid of heat, or the process of making these objects.

ceramic ware   Generally used to refer to table ware made out of ceramic. Also refers to any fired ceramic object.

ceramist   One who makes ceramics.

china   A term usually applied to any white ware fired at a low porcelain temperature. It was developed in Europe to compete with the expensive imported Chinese porcelain.

china clay   Primary clay, or kaolin, that is white, **refractory,** and not very plastic.

china paint   An opaque overglaze paint that is fired onto already-fired glazed ware at various low-range temperatures. Because of the low temperatures used, colors like red or orange do not burn out. Sometimes called **overglaze enamel.**

chuck   An open container used to hold work in place while trimming on the wheel.

clay   A variety of earthy materials formed by the decomposition of granite. In the process, these may have been combined with a variety of other materials, forming clay bodies with differing maturing points.

clay body   See **body.**

coiling   A method of forming pottery or sculpture from rolls of clay melded together to create the walls.

collaring   In wheel throwing, a beginning step in centering a ball of clay on a wheel head. While the wheel head is spinning fast, the potter's hands apply even pressure to the wall of the clay dome causing it to become "true" and centered.

collaring in   In wheel throwing, the technique used to reduce the diameter of a cylinder and to make necks on vases.

coning up   In wheel throwing, a beginning step in centering a lump of clay. While the wheel head is spinning at between approximately 120 and 200 rpm, the clay is forced into a blunt cone shape that "trues" up the clay.

crawling   Crawling is characterized by bare, unglazed areas on fired ceramic ware alternating with thickened glazed areas. Usually caused by surface tension in the molten glaze pulling it away from areas of grease or dust on the surface of the bisque ware.

crazing   Unintentional cracks that occur over the entire glaze surface because the glaze expands and contracts more than the clay body to which it is applied. Caused by improper "fit" of glaze to clay.

cylinder   A clay tube made by forming on the potter's wheel. It can also be made through slab construction around a cardboard, plastic, or metal tube, or a pipe wrapped with a few layers of newspaper, plastic sheeting, or foam, which prevents it from sticking. A cylinder can also be made from an **extruder** machine.

de-airing   Any method of removing air from clay. Wedging de-airs clay to a certain degree, but a pug mill equipped with a de-airing vacuum chamber does a more complete job.

decal   An image or a design printed with ceramic material on a special paper so that it can be transferred to bisque ware or a glazed surface and fired to permanency.

deflocculant   Material such as sodium carbonate or sodium silicate, used in slip for casting to aid in maintaining the fluidity of the slip with less water. Less shrinkage will thus occur in drying the cast object.

die   In ceramics, a metal cut-out through which clay is forced in an extruder, giving it a particular shape. Dies can create solid or hollow extrusions.

dipping   Applying glaze or slip to the object by immersing the piece and shaking off excess glaze.

downdraft kiln   A kiln designed so that the heat moves up through the firing chamber, down through the ware, then is vented into a stack (chimney) opening at the bottom of the kiln.

drape mold   A support (such as a stretched cloth, a wooden frame, or rope network) in or over which a clay slab is draped to shape as it stiffens. The term is also sometimes used for a **hump mold** over which slabs of clay are stiffened.

dry footing   A potters' term for removing all the glaze from the foot of a pot before firing.

drying   The elimination of water from pots and sculpture. Insufficient drying before firing can result in a piece exploding in the kiln, while drying too fast can cause warping or cracking of the ware.

earthenware   Pottery that has been fired at low temperature (below cone 2) and is porous and relatively soft. Usually red or brown in color. Used worldwide for domestic ware, glazed or unglazed.

enamels   Low-temperature opaque or translucent glazes that are usually painted over higher-fired glazed surfaces. Most commonly called **china paints.**

engobe   Originally, the term referred to slip that is applied over the entire surface of a piece of pottery or sculpture to change the color and/or texture of the clay body. The term now often refers to slip used for decoration.

extruder   A mechanical aid for forming moist clay by pressing it through a die. This causes the clay to take the shape of the die. Extruders can form clay quickly into many forms, from tubes to tiles.

feldspar   A group of common rock-forming minerals containing silicates of aluminum, along with potassium, sodium, calcium, and occasionally barium. Used extensively in stoneware and porcelain bodies and in glazes as a flux.

fettling knife   A long, tapered knife used for trimming ware and for cutting slabs.

firebox   The part of the kiln into which fuel is introduced and where combustion takes place.

fire clays (refractory clays)   Clays that withstand high temperatures. Used in kiln bricks and also as ingredients in stoneware bodies or in clay bodies for handbuilding or sculpture.

firing   Heating pottery or sculpture in a kiln or open fire to bring the clay or glaze to **maturity.** The temperature needed to mature a specific clay or glaze varies.

firing chamber   The part of a kiln that holds the ware to be fired.

fit   The adjustment of the glaze composition to the composition of a clay body so that it will adhere to the surface of the ware.

flues   The passageways in a kiln designed to carry the heat from the chamber to the chimney or vent.

flux   In ceramics, flux lowers the melting point of glaze. Oxides such as iron, sodium, potassium, calcium, zinc, lead, boric oxide, and others combine with the silica and other heat-resistant materials in a glaze, helping them to fuse.

foot   The base of a piece of pottery.

frit (fritt)   A glaze material formed when any of several soluble materials are melted together with insoluble materials, cooled rapidly and splintered by immersion in cold water, then ground into a powder. This renders them less soluble and less likely to release toxic materials. Feldspar is a natural frit.

glass former   An essential component of any glaze. The main glass former is silica.

glaze   Any vitreous coating that has been melted onto a clay surface by the use of heat. Made of fine-ground minerals that, when fired to a certain temperature, fuse into a glassy coating. Glazes may be matt or glossy, depending on their components.

glaze firing (also called **glost firing**)   The firing during which glaze materials melt and form a vitreous coating on the clay body surface.

glaze stain   Commercial blends formulated with various coloring oxides that produce a wide range of colors when used in glazes or clay bodies.

greenware   Unfired pottery or sculpture.

grog   Crushed or ground particles of fired clay graded in various sizes of particles. Added to the clay body to help in drying, to add texture, and to reduce shrinkage and warpage.

handbuilding   The process of building pots or sculpture without the use of the potter's wheel. This term includes **pinching** and **coiling** and building with slabs.

high-fire   Describes clays or glazes that are fired from cone 2 up to cone 10 or 13. Ware fired at cone 2 and up is usually considered to be **stoneware. See porcelain.**

high relief   A sculpture whose full contours are almost detached from a flat background.

hump mold   A mold of plaster or terra cotta, or a found object such as a rounded rock, an upended bowl, or a bag of sand, foam padding, or crumpled newspaper over which a slab of clay can be laid to shape as it stiffens.

installation   Ceramic pieces (or any art medium) shown as one work, generally with an overall theme or statement.

kaolin (also called **china clay**)   A white-firing natural clay that withstands high temperatures. An essential ingredient in porcelain.

kick wheel   The traditional potter's wheel which is powered by kicking a lower wheel or by pushing a treadle back and forth with the feet.

kiln   A furnace or an oven built of heat-resistant materials for firing pottery or sculpture.

kiln furniture   Heat-resistant shelves, posts, and slabs that support the ware in the kiln during firing. Kiln shelves may warp in firing if they are not well supported.

kiln sitter   A control that uses small **pyrometric cones** that slump when the desired temperature is reached and turn off power to an electric kiln by tripping a switch or in a gas kiln by shutting off the gas solenoid valve.

kiln wash   A coating of refractory materials (half flint and half kaolin) painted onto the kiln floor and the top side of shelves to keep the melting glaze from fusing the ware onto the shelves.

latex   An emulsion of rubber or plastic material with water. Used in ceramics as a resist material in applying glazes.

lead   Until recently, when the solubility of lead in acid foods and liquids was understood, lead was used as a low-fire or medium-temperature flux in glazes. Potters now do not use lead in any glaze for containers that can be used for food or liquid.

leather-hard   The condition of a clay body when much of the moisture has evaporated and shrinkage has just ended, but the clay is not totally dry. Carving, burnishing, or joining slabs is often done at this stage.

lip (or rim)   The edge of the opening of a pot.

local reduction   Creation of a **reduction** atmosphere in one section of a kiln or in a **sagger** through direct contact with combustible material.

low-fire   The range of firing of clays and glazes in which the kiln temperature reached is usually in the cone 015 to cone 1 range.

low relief   See **bas-relief.**

luster (lustre)   A thin film of metallic salts usually, though not always, applied to a glazed surface, then refired at a low temperature in reduction. Modern luster mediums include a reducing material.

maiolica (majolica)   The Italian name for tin-glaze ware that was sent from Spain to Italy via the island of Majorca. Later, local styles of decoration were developed in Italian pottery towns such as Faenza and Deruta. Now a general term for any earthenware covered with a tin-lead glaze.

maquette   In sculpture, a French term used for quick, small preliminary sketches.

matt glaze   A glaze with a dull, nonglossy finish due to its deliberate composition. Alumina added to the glaze, along with a slow cooling, assists the formation of matt glazes.

maturing point (maturity)   Refers to the temperature and time in firing at which a clay or glaze reaches the desired condition of hardness and density. Both clays and glazes have differing maturing points, depending on their composition.

mixed media   In ceramics, the combining of various media, such as metal, wood, paper, stone, with clay in pottery or sculpture.

model   The original form in clay, plaster, wood, plastic, metal, or other material from which a mold is made.

modeling   In sculpture, the act of giving three-dimensional form and detail to plastic clay, using fingers or tools.

mold   Any form that can be used to shape fluid or plastic substances. In ceramics, usually the negative form from which pottery or sculpture can be cast by pouring or pressing methods using either liquid slip or damp clay. Molds can be made in one piece or in multiple sections. See also **hump mold.**

multipart mold   See **piece mold.**

multiples   A series of identical objects usually referring to those formed in **molds.**

neck   The area of a pot that narrows in near the top before it flares out to the opening.

needle tool   A tool with a fine tip, like a needle. Used for cutting, **scoring** and **trimming.**

opacifier   A material that causes a glaze to become opaque by producing minute crystals. Tin, zirconium, and titanium oxides are used as opacifiers in combination with various oxides.

opening   The process of making a hole in a centered ball of clay while the wheel is spinning medium to fast. The first step is to make a hole in the clay dome 1 to 2 in. (25 to 50 mm) wide and ¼ to ½ in. (6 to 13 mm) from the bottom. The second step is to widen the opening by pulling the wall out.

overglaze   Often called **enamel** or **china paint.** A low-temperature ceramic enamel painted on a previously glazed and fired surface, then fired for a second time at a lower temperature, usually as the final firing process used to obtain bright colors like red and orange that would burn out at high temperatures will be maintained in the lower firing.

oxidation (oxidizing firing)   The firing of a kiln or open fire with complete combustion so that the firing atmosphere contains enough oxygen to allow the metals in clays and glazes to produce their oxide colors. Electric kilns always produce oxidizing firings unless reducing materials are added. Bright and clear low-fire colors are associated with glazes and clays fired in an oxidation atmosphere.

oxide   A combination of an element with oxygen. In ceramics, oxides are used in formulating and coloring glazes and clay bodies. They are also used in solution with water for decorating ware.

peephole (or spyhole)   A hole in the door or wall of a kiln through which the ceramist can watch the pyrometric cones, the color of heat in the kiln, and the process of the firing. (Always wear goggles of the proper shade [#3 to #5] when peering into a kiln through a peephole.)

piece mold (or multipart mold)   A mold for casting that is made in sections so that it can be removed easily from the cast object without distortion. Generally used to cast an object that has undercuts and that therefore cannot be removed from a one-piece mold.

pinching   In ceramics, the act of squeezing plastic clay between thumb and finger to form a pot or sculpture.

pinholes   Small holes in a glaze caused by the bursting of blisters formed by gases as they escape through the glaze during firing.

pit (or open) firing   The firing of greenware that is either piled on the ground or placed in a shallow pit with combustible material surrounding the ware. Used worldwide in pre-industrial societies, and today often used by potters to achieve color variation due to uneven combustion.

pithos (plural, pithoi)   A greek term for a large storage jar made of earthenware.

plaster   A white powder prepared from gypsum which becomes a dense absorbent mass when added to water. In ceramics, plaster of Paris or Pottery Plaster #1 are used to make **slip-casting molds** or **press molds.**

plaster mold   A mold made of plaster that is primarily used for slip-cast molds because of its ability to absorb large amounts of moisture from the clay. Compared to wood, plastic, or concrete, plaster molds have superior absorption properties. **Press** and **drape** molds are also made of plaster.

plastic clay   A particularly malleable **clay body** used for **throwing** on the wheel.

plasticity   The ability of a damp clay body to yield under pressure without cracking and to retain the formed shape after the pressure is released.

platelets (clay)   The basic particles of clay.

porcelain   A translucent, nonabsorbent body fired at high temperature. White and hard, it was first developed in China. Traditionally fired in the 2370°–2640°F (1300°–1450°C) range, some porcelain bodies have been developed that mature in the 2230°–2340°F (1220°–1280°C) range.

post-firing fuming   Low temperature methods to heat ceramic, sprayed with sulfates or combined with materials and chemicals such as copper carbonate, seaweed, banana peels, pine needles, or newspaper, for the purpose of changing or adding color to the surface.

potter's wheel   A revolving wheel, powered by foot or by electricity, on which clay is shaped into pottery. (See also **centrifugal force**).

pottery   Originally a term for earthenware, now loosely used to refer to any type of ceramic ware, as well as to the workshop where it is made.

pouring   In ceramics, pouring can mean either pouring slip into a mold or applying glaze to a pot by pouring the glaze over the outside or into the interior.

press mold   Any mold made from plaster, fired clay, wood, or a found object into which damp clay can be pressed to reproduce the shape of the mold.

primary clay   Clay found in nature that was formed in place rather than transported by the action of water. Also called residual clay. Kaolin is a primary clay.

pulling a handle   A method to make handles for cups, lids, or containers by pulling and stretching the clay. A clay slug is held vertically, wetted, and pulled many times, stretching the piece into a long round or oval tapered coil. It is then cut into pieces and made into handles.

pulling up   In making pottery on a wheel, the process of raising the cylinder wall using both hands and fingers. The potter gently squeezes with equal pressure on the wall while moving upward, and the clay begins to rise.

pyrometer   A device for measuring and recording the exact interior temperature of a kiln throughout the firing and cooling process.

pyrometric cones   Small pyramids of ceramic materials formulated to bend over and melt at designated temperatures. Orton cones in the United States and Seger cones in England and Europe have different ranges.

quartz inversion point   The point at which the silica crystals in clay change in structure and volume during the rise and fall of the temperature in the kiln. This development influences the fit of glaze to clay body.

raku   Originally a name used by a Japanese family that made tea ceremony ware. Now refers to the process of raku firing and to ware glazed in such a firing. Raku ware is often reduced after firing by burying it in combustible material, then covering it with an airtight lid. This reduction atmosphere aids in producing luster or opalescent colors.

reduction (reducing firing, reduction atmosphere)   A firing in which insufficient air is supplied to the kiln for complete combustion. Under these conditions, the carbon monoxide in the kiln combines with the oxygen in the oxides of the clay body and glaze, causing the oxides to change color. Commonly associated with high-fired stoneware, porcelain, raku, and lusters.

refractory   Resistance to heat and melting. Refractory materials are used in porcelain and stoneware. Also used for building kilns and kiln furniture and in combination with other materials, as kiln insulation.

relief   The projection of forms from a flat background in sculpture or decoration. The terms **high relief** and **low relief** describe the amount of projection above the background.

resist   A method of applying a covering material such as wax, latex, stencils, or masking tape to bisque or glazed ware, then coating the piece with a slip, a glaze, or a second glaze. The resist material will not accept the added layer so that on firing, the color of the covered area will remain intact.

rib   A curved tool made of wood, metal, or plastic, used for shaping, scraping, or smoothing clay objects.

ribbing   Use of a **rib** to shape or smooth moist clay, or scrape damp or dry clay.

rim (or lip)   The edge of the opening of a pot.

sagger   A heat resistant container in which **ware** is placed to protect it from the fire. Also used for **local reduction,** generally in kilns, by placing organic material in the **sagger** with the ware.

salt glaze   A glaze formed by introducing salt into a hot kiln. The vaporized salt combines with the silica in the clay body, forming a sodium silicate glaze on the surface. Salt glazing releases noxious and toxic fumes, so many potters now use alternatives.

scoring   Scratching or otherwise roughening the edges of damp or leather-hard clay before joining them.

scoring tool   A tool used for **scoring** the clay. Usually has several prongs to create multiple scoring. Generally used when joining clay forms.

secondary clay   Natural clay that has been moved by water or wind from its source and settled elsewhere in deposits.

sgraffito   Decoration of pottery made by scratching through a layer of colored slip to the differently colored clay body underneath.

shoulder   The upper curved area of a pot or vessel that usually begins at the outer perimeter of the wall and angles inward.

shrinkage   The loss of volume in clay as it shrinks in drying or in firing. Shrinkage varies from 7 percent to 20 percent from wet clay to fired clay, depending on the clay.

sieve   A utensil of wire mesh (usually brass to resist rust) used to strain liquids or powdered materials.

silica   Oxide of silicon, SiO_2. Found in nature as quartz or flint sand, it is the most common of all ceramic materials.

silicate of soda   A solution of sodium silicate that is used as a **deflocculant** to help in the suspension of clay materials in slip.

slab roller   A mechanical device for rolling out slabs to a set, consistent thickness.

slip   A suspension of clay in water used for casting pottery or sculpture in molds. Slip (sometimes called **engobe**) can also be used for painted decoration or for the **sgraffito** technique.

slip casting   Forming objects by pouring slip into a plaster mold. The mold absorbs the water in the slip so that solid clay walls are formed to create a positive of the original.

slip glaze A glaze that contains a large proportion of clay. Generally one that contains enough flux to form a glaze with few or no additives.

slip trailer A rubber syringe used to apply decorations of slip on ware.

slurry A thick, creamy mixture of clay and water.

spray booth A ventilated booth that removes chemicals and fumes from the air so that the person spraying does not inhale them while spraying glazes, underglazes, or overglazes.

spray gun A gun-like device through which compressed air passes, forcing the substance into a fine mist for application. Used for spraying glazes.

spraying In ceramics, the method of applying a glaze by using a spray gun.

sprigging The process of attaching low-relief decorations of damp clay onto already formed **greenware.**

spyhole See **peephole.**

stains Commercially processed and refined raw chemicals that yield ceramic stains and offer a wide range of shades for coloring clays and glazes. They are generally more color stable than oxides.

stilts Triangular supports with either clay (for low-fire) or heat-resistant metal points (for low- or high-fire), used to support pieces of glazed pottery above the shelves during glaze firing to keep the glaze from sticking the ware to the shelf. Small stilt marks can be filed, sanded, or ground smooth.

stoneware A type of clay body fired to a temperature at which the body becomes vitrified, dense, and nonabsorptive, but not translucent. Usually matures at temperatures above 2192°F (1200°C).

temper Any material, such as sand, mica, or crushed fired pottery fragments (**grog**), added to a clay body to make it more porous and less likely to shrink and warp.

tenmoku (temmoku, tienmu) High-fired, saturated iron glaze; black, brown, and yellowish. Used by the Chinese and Japanese, especially on tea ware. Still a popular glaze.

terra-cotta A low-fire, porous, reddish clay body, frequently containing grog or other temper. Used throughout history for common, utilitarian ware; also used for sculpture.

terra sigillata A fine slip glaze. Used by the Greeks, Etruscans, and Romans to coat their pottery. Now formulated in a wide variety of colors.

test tiles Small tiles made of clay used to test clay bodies in the kiln or to test glazes on a specific clay body.

thermal shock The stress to which ceramic material is subjected when sudden changes occur in the heat during firing or cooling.

thermocouple A long probe connected to a temperature gauge called a pyrometer by wires that transfer the temperature measured inside a kiln.

throwing Forming objects on the potter's wheel using a clay body with plastic qualities (see **plasticity**).

trailing A method of decorating in which a slip or glaze is squeezed out of a syringe, or **slip trailer.**

trimming In ceramics, this refers to trimming excess clay off the foot and sometimes the body of a pot to refine the shape.

undercut A negative space in a solid form, creating an overhang. Casting a form with undercutting requires a multipart mold in order to release the mold from the cast.

underfire To fire clay or glaze—accidentally or deliberately—to a point below its maturing point. Underfiring can turn a normally glossy glaze into a matt surface.

underglaze Any coloring material used under a glaze. The color can be provided by oxides or by commercially prepared glaze and clay body **stains.**

updraft kiln A kiln in which the heat goes up through the chamber and is vented through the top of the kiln.

vitreous Having the nature of glass. In ceramics, a glaze or clay body that has been fired to a dense, hard, and nonabsorbent condition. High-fire glazes vitrify and combine with the glassy particles that form in the high-fire clay body as it approaches vitrification. This results in a glaze that is united with the clay body as compared to a low-fire glaze that merely coats the surface of the fired clay.

vitrification The state of being vitrified, or glassy.

ware A general term applied to any ceramic—**earthenware, stoneware,** or **porcelain**—in the green, bisqued, or fired state.

warping Changes in the form of a clay body. Warping of ware can occur during drying or firing if the walls are built unevenly or if drying or firing is too rapid or uneven.

wax resist A method of decoration in which melted wax or oil emulsion is painted onto the clay body or onto a glazed piece. See **resist.**

wedging Any one of various methods of kneading a mass of clay to expel the air, get rid of lumps, and prepare a homogenous material.

wedging table A table of plaster, wood, or concrete, often covered with canvas, on which clay can be wedged. A stretched wire attached to the table allows one to cut the clay to check for air bubbles, lumps, or lack of homogeneity.

well In wheel throwing, the opening in the centered ball of clay. The initial opening is made by pushing down the middle of the clay dome with fingers or thumbs. To widen the well, the potter pulls the wall horizontally, stretching the clay.

Further Reading

HISTORY

Barnett, William K., and John W. Hoopes, Eds. Washington and London: The Smithsonian Institution Press, 1995.

China, Japan

Cardozo, Sidney B., and Masaaki Hitano. *The Art of Rosanjin*. New York: Kodansha, 1987.

Cort, Louise. *Shigaraki Potter's Valley*. New York: Kodansha, 1980.

Leach, Bernard. *A Potter in Japan*. London: Faber & Faber, 1960.

Medley, Margaret. *The Chinese Potter*. Ithaca, N.Y.: Cornell University Press, 1982.

Medley, Margaret. *The Chinese Potter: A Practical History of Chinese Ceramics*. 3rd ed. London: Phaidon Press, 1999.

Peterson, Susan. *Shoiji Hamada: A Potter's Way and Work*. New York: Kodansha, 1982.

Africa

Barley, Nigel. *Smashing Pots: Feats of Clay from Africa*. London: British Museum Press, 1994.

Bartlett, John. *English Decorative Ceramics*. London: Kevin Francis Publishing, 1989.

Gebauer, Paul. *Art of Cameroon*. Portland, Oregon, and New York: Portland Art Museum and Metropolitan Museum of Art, 1979.

Hildyard, Robin. *European Ceramics*. Philadelphia: University of Pennsylvania Press, 1999.

The Americas

Clark, Garth, and Margie Hughto. *A Century of Ceramics in the United States, 1878–1978*. New York: Dutton and Everson Museum of Art, 1979.

Coe, Michael D. *The Maya*. New York, London: Thames and Hudson, 1985.

Lackey, Luana M. *The Pottery of Acatlan: A Changing Mexican Tradition*. Tucson: University of Arizona Press, 1982.

Levin, Elaine. *The History of American Ceramics*. New York: Abrams, 1988.

Litto, Gertrude. *South American Folk Pottery*. New York: Watson-Guptill, 1976.

Peterson, Susan. *The Living Tradition of Maria Martinez*. New York: Kodansha, 1981.

Europe

Carnegy, Daphne. *Tin-Glazed Earthenware: From Maiolica, Faience and Delftware to the Contemporary*. London: A & C Black and Radnor, Pa.: Chilton Book Co., 1993.

GENERAL

Berensohn, Paulus. *Finding One's Way with Clay*. Dallas: Bisquit Books, 1997.

Chavarria, Joaquim. *The Big Book of Ceramics*. New York: Watson-Guptill, 1994.

Fournier, Robert. *Illustrated Dictionary of Practical Pottery*. 3rd edition. Radnor, Pa.: Chilton Book Co., 1992.

Giorgini, Frank. *Handmade Tiles: Designing, Making, Decorating*. Asheville, N.C.: Lark Books, 1994.

Munsterberg, Hugo, and Marjorie Munsterberg. *World Ceramics: From Prehistoric to Modern Times*. New York: Penguin Studio, 1998.

Pancioli, Diana. *Extruded Ceramics: Techniques, Projects, Inspirations*. New York: Lark Books, 2000.

Peterson, Susan. *The Craft and Art of Clay*. Englewood Cliffs, N.J.: Prentice-Hall, 1992.

Peterson, Susan. *Working with Clay: An Introduction*. Woodstock, N.Y.: The Overlook Press, 1998.

Piepenburg, Robert. *The Spirit of Clay*. Farmington Hills, Mich.: Pebble Press, 1996.

Richards, M. C. *Centering in Pottery, Poetry and the Person*. Middletown, Conn.: Wesleyan University Press, 1964.

Speight, Charlotte, and John Toki. *Hands in Clay.* 3rd edition. Mountain View, Calif.: Mayfield, 1994.

Yanagi, Soetsu. *The Unknown Craftsman.* New York: Kodansha, 1989.

Zakin, Richard. *Ceramics: Mastering the Craft.* Radnor, Pa.: Chilton Book Co., 1990.

SURFACES

Constant, Christine, and Steve Ogden. *The Potter's Palette.* Radnor, Pa.: Chilton Book Co., 1996.

Hinchcliffe, John, and Wendy Barber. *Ceramic Style: Making and Decorating Patterned Ceramic Ware.* London: Cassell, 1998.

Hopper, Robin. *The Ceramic Spectrum.* Radnor, Pa.: Chilton Book Co., 1984.

Peters, Ivan. *Surface Decoration for Low-Fire Ceramics.* Asheville, N.C.: Lark Books, 1999.

Scott, Paul. *Ceramics and Print.* Philadelphia: University of Pennsylvania Press, 1995.

Wilson, Lana. *Ceramics: Shape and Surface.* n.p., 1997.

Zakin, Richard. *Electric Kiln Ceramics: A Potter's Guide to Clay and Glazes.* 2nd edition. London: A & C Black and Radnor, Pa.: Chilton Book Co., 1994.

KILNS AND FIRING

Andrews, Tim. *Raku: A Review of Contemporary Work.* Radnor, Pa.: Chilton Book Co., 1994.

Branfman, Steve. *Raku: A Practical Approach.* Radnor, Pa.: Chilton Book Co., 1991.

Olsen, Frederick L. *The Kiln Book.* 2nd edition. Radnor, Pa.: Chilton Book Co., 1983.

Rice, Prudence M., ed. *The Prehistory and History of Ceramic Kilns,* vol. 7, *Ceramics and Civilization,* ed. W. D. Kingery. Westerville, Ohio: The American Ceramic Society, 1997.

SCULPTURE

Grubbs, Daisy. *Modeling a Likeness in Clay.* New York: Watson-Guptill Publications, 1982.

Grubbs, Daisy. *Modeling a Likeness in Clay.* New York: Watson-Guptill, 1992.

Peck, Judith. *Sculpture as Experience: Working with Clay, Wire, Wax, Plaster and Found Objects.* Radnor, Pa.: Chilton Book Co., 1989.

Plowman, John. *The Encyclopedia of Sculpting Techniques.* Philadelphia, London: Running Press, 1995.

Speight, Charlotte. *Images in Clay Sculpture: Historical and Contemporary Techniques.* New York: Harper & Row, 1983.

Triplett, Kathy. *Handbuilt Ceramics.* New York: Lark Books, 1997.

MOLDS

Colclough, John. *Mould Making.* Florida: Gentle Breeze Publishing, 1999.

Frith, Donald. *Moldmaking for Ceramics.* Radnor, Pa.: Chilton Book Co. and London: A & C Black, 1992.

Peirce, Clayton. *The Clay Lover's Guide to Making Molds: Designing, Making, Using.* Asheville, N.C.: Lark Books, 1998.

SAFETY

McCann, Michael. *Artist Beware! The Hazards and Precautions in Working with Art and Craft Materials.* New York: Watson-Guptill, 1979.

Rossol, Monona. *Keeping Clay Work Safe and Legal.* 2nd ed. n.p.: Wayne County Press in cooperation with National Council on Education for the Ceramic Arts, 1996.

Seeger, Nancy. *A Ceramist's Guide to the Safe Use of Materials.* Chicago: School of the Art Institute of Chicago, 1984.

Index